Modern Dance in a Postmodern World

AN ANALYSIS OF FEDERAL ARTS FUNDING AND ITS IMPACT ON THE FIELD OF MODERN DANCE

Jan Van Dyke

National Dance Association
an association of the
**American Alliance for Health,
Physical Education, Recreation and Dance**

Cover credit: Photo of Kathryn Posin Dance Company by Lois
Greenfield. Design by Bernie Amtmann, Plus Design

ISBN 0-88314-525-1

Purposes of the
American Alliance for Health, Physical
Education, Recreation and Dance

The American Alliance is an educational organization, structured for the purposes of supporting, encouraging, and providing assistance to member groups and their personnel throughout the nation as they seek to initiate, develop, and conduct programs in health, leisure, and movement-related activities for the enrichment of human life.

Alliance objectives include:

1. Professional growth and development—to support, encourage, and provide guidance in the development and conduct of programs in health, leisure, and movement-related activities which are based on the needs, interests, and inherent capacities of the individual in today's society.

2. Communication—to facilitate public and professional understanding and appreciation of health, leisure, and movement-related activities, and to disseminate the findings to the profession and other interested and concerned publics.

3. Standards and guidelines—to further the continuous development and evaluation of standards within the profession for personnel and programs in health, leisure, and movement-related activities.

4. Public affairs—to coordinate and administer a planned program of professional, public, and governmental relations that will improve education in areas of health, leisure, and movement-related activities.

5. To conduct such other activities as shall be approved by the Board of Governors and the Alliance Assembly, provided that the Alliance shall not engage in any activity which would be inconsistent with the status of an educational and charitable organization as defined in Section 501(c)(3) of the Internal Revenue Code of 1954 or any successor provision thereto, and none of the said purposes shall at any time be deemed or construed to be purposes other than the public benefit purposes and objectives consistent with such educational and charitable status.

Contents

Jan Van Dyke—1976
of Jan Van Dyke & Dancers
in rehearsal

Preface

When I graduated from the University of Wisconsin and entered the dance world, it was the early 1960s. I knew how to dance, because I had been dancing for many years, but I knew very little else about the field. As a dance student, I had had no interest in teaching or choreographing. My ideas about the arts were idealistic and my knowledge of how the dance world operated, non-existent. During the 1960s and 1970s I worked and studied in New York for four years altogether, but concentrated most of my energy on Washington, DC. It was not long before I realized that if I wanted to be a dancer in a city like Washington, I would have to create opportunities for myself, and that meant learning to choreograph and beginning to teach. At that point I went back to school for an MA to learn those skills, and I gradually set about working: teaching and running a studio, teaching in other people's studios and in local university dance programs, operating a performance space, and most of all, choreographing and performing with my company, Jan Van Dyke & Dancers in and around the mid-Atlantic region. I experienced the 1970s as a powerful, booming time for dance.

With the onset of the 1980s, however, it was clear that times were changing, and I was growing older. During that decade I left Washington to spend two years teaching and performing in New York City again, and followed that with three years in the San Francisco Bay Area. Finally, in 1986, I enrolled in a doctoral program at the University of North Carolina at Greensboro. Though I had been unable to verbalize it, I knew my experience of dance and dancing was changing and I turned to academia for some time out and the opportunity to think things through. Back in school, with distance from the daily readiness of life in the field, I reflected on influences as diverse as the Judson Dance Theater and federal funding policies, and as they came into focus, I connected them to my experiences as a dance artist.

When I first encountered the democratic, egalitarian ideals of the Judson Dance Theater, they could not have been further from the beliefs I held. I saw Yvonne Rainer's "Trio A" as part of "Rose Fractions" at the Billy Rose Theater in New York City in 1969. At the time, the work was completely foreign to my eye. All around me, the audience was excited, and I knew, as I watched, that I lacked some key or code to understanding what I was seeing.

My early teachers had been students and dancers with Graham, Humphrey, and Wigman. For them, dance was a means of theater, filled with expression, unified with an organic, musical flow, and best done by skilled dancers. In both class and rehearsal, I danced with a spiritual energy, certain that dance was an empowering, life-giving force, of which I desperately wanted to be worthy. At that point, to me, "Trio A" appeared formless, certainly without style or technique, and so without meaning. I had no way to approach it, it was so alien to my concepts of dance and dancing. What I did not know then was that "Trio A" would eventually come to represent the viewpoint of an entire era, and as such, would become part of my consciousness as well. Though I could not have predicted it, my ideas of what dance should be would grow with the times, to embrace a broad spectrum of aesthetic possibilities.

On the other hand, by the time I became a doctoral student, I had known for some time that American society was changing and that dance was being shaped by forces distinctly of the culture—my work along with it. I had first become aware of these changes in the early 1980s, while living in California, when I went to introduce myself and my dance company to a local foundation. There I was told that they were not interested in seeing my work as such: "We're not into making aesthetic judgments," they said. Instead, they wanted to see my company balance sheets. In other words, they would let the marketplace be the judge of whether my work merited support: If my company was stable and showing potential for growth, I became interesting to them.

Coming away from this meeting, I was struck by the paradox that trapped me. With a small company new to the Bay Area, I was looking for funding to establish myself in the region and to lend legitimacy to my work and my group. I was trying to build a reputation. Funding agencies, on the other hand, were looking for established groups who already had reputations, and they relied on a company's business records to tell them who merited support. During the months that followed, I reflected on the shift I perceived, a shift that pushed me to think more about my work as a product, something to market. The establishment of an objective criterion such as balance sheets seemed an ironic development, counter to the experimental, almost religious values I had come to associate with modern dance.

I was not the only one who detected a shift. At about the same time, a friend, with her own company, expressed concern that all her dancers dress in suits and high heels to meet prospective board members. "Why?" I asked. "You are asking them [the board members] to enter our world; perhaps they should see us as we really are." Her response was clear: "No, it's the reverse," she said. "We are trying to enter their world."

These experiences speak of the changing nature of modern dance during the 1980s and the relation of art to American society — and led eventually to the ideas which form the central theme of this text: the interrelationship of economics and aesthetics in the American culture. Historically, modern dancers have led a marginal economic existence. During the 1960s and early 1970s, most accepted borderline poverty as the price to be paid for involvement in the arts, and so maintained an outsider's perspective on the society in which they worked. Since the 1980s, however, my sense is that many artists have acquired values more in accord with mainstream American culture and have come to see popular acclaim and financial stability as an index of success. This shift, linked inextricably to the National Endowment for the Arts and other funding agencies, has fundamentally changed the nature of careers in dance and the way in which many choreographers approach their work.

The argument briefly stated above is developed over four chapters, with a fifth to sum it up. The first chapter provides a broad historical background to modern dance with the aim of showing, through the lives of seminal dance artists, what might be called a modern dance point of view. This point of view can be seen as having a critical and revolutionary perspective, one which I believe largely ceased to exist in the 1980s. My view is that the shift in the stance of dance artists reflects the impact of cultural forces, most particularly the catalytic influence of the funding policies of major foundations and the federal government.

The historical survey here is far from exhaustive. There are many complex issues and crosscurrents that could not be addressed. However, one thread I have tried to carry through the chapter is the economic situation for dancers, in preparation for a later examination of what changes in this area have been achieved, and the ways in which the financial aspect of the field has interacted with the experience of dance artists and their philosophical and artistic concerns.

Chapter II examines the National Endowment for the Arts, the largest and most influential funding agency in this country, focusing on its role as a catalyst for change and as a policy-maker for funding agencies nationwide. There is a brief background description of the founding of the NEA and then a discussion of the influence the agency has had on the organizational structure of dance companies, on their financial stability, and on the decentralization of the modern dance field. In addition, the impact of federal funding patterns on other grant-making agencies and the nature of the funding process itself are examined. The chapter concludes with a discussion of the political implications of NEA funding policies both on American society and on dance.

In an effort to illustrate the subjective nature of knowledge and to gain insights from individual experience, Chapter III presents interviews with four dance artists actively involved in the field during the period discussed in Chapter II, touching on their histories and their views on dance in the late 1980s. Given the scope and range of the modern dance field today, this is not meant to be a representative sampling, but an attempt to describe the experience of individual dance artists coping with a changing world, giving theoretical concerns a human aspect. What is revealed is both the diversity of personal response to a shared cultural environment and the extent of the dialogue between culture and the individual.

The people selected are colleagues I have known over the course of my career. They range in age from forty-five to fifty at the time of the interviews. They can speak from experience about changes in the field which have affected their lives and their work. All four are modern dancers and all are college graduates. I purposely chose articulate, thoughtful people with developed points of view, able to discuss their experience in some depth.

Each was interviewed once for about one and one-half hours. For each, there were then follow-up questions by telephone, catching details which had slipped by me. The interviews themselves were loosely structured. I began with a description of the scope of my study and then asked each one to start by talking about his or her life in the 1960s. I asked them to concentrate on their experience of the dance field with an emphasis on the economic-creative axis, and how they have adapted over the years. Otherwise, I allowed the talk to range, and in a sense, what each says is determined by what he or she considered primary.

I met Elizabeth Keen for the first time in 1971, when, for six weeks, we found ourselves neighbors in a college dormitory while on the faculty at the Long Beach Summer School of Dance in California. Since then, I have taught with her, briefly, at Ohio University, produced her company in concert in Washington, DC, and performed in her work both in California and New York.

My acquaintance with Kathryn Posin began in the late 1960s when John Gamble and I co-directed the Georgetown Workshop, a small studio-theater and repertory dance company in Washington, DC. We were always looking for new work to perform. Our legal counsel was my brother Jon, who, at the time, was on the Law Faculty at Catholic University. One of his colleagues was a Dan Posin, who, it seemed, had a sister just starting out as a choreographer in New York City. In 1968, on the recommendation of her brother, we invited Kathy to set a dance on our company. It was one of my first links to the New York dance world and the beginning of a long acquaintance.

I met Spider Kedelsky in New York around 1970 when he was still known as Harold Silver. He was working with Rudy Perez at the time. Our paths have crossed over the years, but we have not known each other well until the 1988–1989 school year when we both found ourselves teaching in the dance department at UNC/Greensboro.

Jefferson James and I both attended Mount Vernon High School in Fairfax County, Virginia during the 1950s. Though we were growing up in different dance studios, we knew each other from afar as fellow dancers. After high school graduation, I was not to see her again for nearly ten years, until 1968, when she came backstage after a performance at the Georgetown Workshop and introduced herself. Since then, we have worked together every year or two: first, when she joined us at the Georgetown Workshop for a year, and since, when I have been invited to teach and/or set work on her Cincinnati company.

Throughout the course of this writing, I have become conscious of my own evolution as a thinker and an artist, particularly since re-entering the academic world. After a twenty year career as a dance professional, I am aware of shifts within my own point of view as I spend more and more time pursuing scholarly concerns. This was of particular interest to me during the writing of the third chapter, filled as it is with reminders of the meaning which being a dance professional gives to life: the financial uncertainty, the ongoing pressure of justifying one's point of view and selling one's work, the fickleness and the power of the institutional dance world—the funders, the press, the producers; the almost religious devotion needed to sustain a career and the sacrifices required to maintain oneself as an active artist.

The fourth chapter, which focuses on dance and education, serves to underline the inevitability of the shift in my perspective, and yet I continue to be surprised. For example, in the dance world, the skill of dancing has always been of primary importance, to the exclusion of most other possibilities. Though now, with an EdD and three years as a dance professor, I see the narrowness of this emphasis, I am reminded daily by my students and my professional friends that dancing is what counts. Not two weeks after I had finished writing in Chapter IV of my concern about the BFA degree and my hope that liberal arts colleges will continue to exert an influence within the field, a dancer friend of mine—an intelligent, successful, ballet-trained New York performer with no college degree—referred to Sarah Lawrence College as a place where they educate dilettantes. Probably, conservatory-style training is what she considers best. For many years I had no problem with it myself. Now, however, I worry that the profession is leaning toward this kind of training, and I wonder at the effect on choreography and on thinking within the field. Dancers in the early companies of Graham and Humphrey were, on the whole, mature individuals when they began their studies, which limited the development of technical skills, but did not hinder the choreography of masterworks.

There are other instances where I have found myself at odds with the prevailing view: while visiting Elizabeth Keen recently, I accompanied her to Juilliard to watch her work with a freshman composition class. The students were all exceptionally well-trained and carefully selected for ability and body type. As I watched them work, mentally I compared them with my students at the University of North Carolina at Greensboro who, though they are good students, go through no entrance audition, and so are much more varied in their looks, abilities, and dance backgrounds. During a break, Liz came over with a comment about the technique of the Juilliard students and how they were a choreographer's dream—didn't they make me drool? But I had been thinking the opposite, that I found their sameness bland and their supple elasticity lacking in texture and character. Some, perhaps many, will go on to notable professional careers. I, however, was aware of looking for interesting and character-giving limitations, and of a desire to see energy, effort, and human-ness in their dancing.

For me, now, the links between education and leadership are self-evident. It seems inescapable that current attitudes about dance education relate to what I perceive as a vacuum within the dance field: a lack of resonant leadership in a time of crisis. The demand for more and better technique seems to be increasing. Just as with sports records, we are no longer satisfied with what was possible thirty years ago. Much influence lately has come from the world of business, from administrators and managers who bring business values and ethics to the fore, making us aware of the economic consequences of artistic decisions. This is an issue I would not have voiced as a professional choreographer; now, in writing about the field, it seems important to both artistic and social concerns.

I have not always thought this way and wonder if, in educating myself, I have also separated myself from the aesthetics and ethics of the field I have known so well. A professor once described education as a socialization process which makes it impossible to go home again. From here, I can understand what that means.

For their part in helping with this text, I would like to express my gratitude to David Purpel for his guidance, to Sue Stinson for the encouragement she gave and the example she set, to John Gamble for pointing me in this direction, and to Liz, Kathy, Spider, and Jeff, many thanks.

JAN VAN DYKE

The Paul Taylor Dance Company
in "Mercuric Tidings"

I

The Modern Dance
Point of View

The Origins of Modern Dance

Modern dance had its beginnings in revolution, and throughout the years, has maintained that kind of tradition, breaking the form at approximately thirty year intervals. It is an art which has, from the beginning, chosen to speak to its own time and locale. This has required a constant and recurring rebellion against the work of previous generations. Custom has only had to make an appearance, to hint at establishing itself, and the next generation has redefined the form. The history of modern dance has been a history of reconception. The field has consistently sought significance in the contemporary world, maintaining a critical eye to its own development, guarding against stagnation and codification, and protecting its belief in the individual vision. The approach is almost anti-historical, with each generation creating the world anew, discarding the hard won tenets of those who went before.

1

Before the advent of modern dance, the United States had no concept of dance as a native art form. During the eighteenth and nineteenth centuries, American ballet looked to Europe for its style, standards, goals, and performers (Ruyter, 1979, p. 9). Theatrical dance in this country existed in a subculture within the working class, well outside the bounds of respectability. American theatrical dancers were generally the children of theater people, the urban poor, or farmers, and they were taught to the European model by European teachers. Because of low salaries, 19th century chorus dancers often worked in factories or restaurants on the side. Neither ballet nor its counterparts, vaudeville and minstrel shows, seriously engaged the moral, political, or social leadership of this country before the 20th century. Prominent citizens may have attended performances, but as far as we know, they did not subsidize the work, argue its virtues, marry dancers, or encourage their children in theatrical careers (Ruyter, p. 10).

During the first two decades of the twentieth century, the United States persisted in discounting its own artists, forcing many to look to Europe for recognition. On that continent, the decades surrounding the turn of the century were years of artistic growth and excitement. At the end of the 1800s, the Impressionists had had a strong impact on the world of painting, opening up new vistas in color and composition and spawning innovation and debate throughout the Western art world. In dance, Serge Diaghilev had formed the Ballet Russes (1909–1929), exposing Europe to Russian ballet while bringing that form into the modern world through collaborations with great artists from many media, among them, Pablo Picasso, Igor Stravinsky, Jean Cocteau, and Vaslav Nijinsky.

The question of an American dance art was first raised by two different American dancers: Isadora Duncan and Ruth St. Denis. Both did much of their work in the first decade of this century, ahead of Diaghilev's influence. As American artists, both had gone to Europe to work, to establish and validate their reputations. As it developed, Duncan stayed and St. Denis returned to the United States.

Both advocated freedom as a means to art and spirituality and each raised the status of dance by taking on the role of philosopher, writing and speaking about the form. They were the first who refused to adapt to what was, and with a vision of what the art might be, reshaped its course. By outlining the great truths they saw hidden in nature and expressing the ideal beauty inherent in natural forms, by connecting the physical with the spiritual, Duncan and St. Denis gave dance a moral function and made it essentially religious.

Duncan's rebellion was against the strictures of ballet, against its formalism and its technique, which she saw as unnatural:

> ... the ballet of today, vainly striving against the natural laws of gravitation or the natural will of the individual, and working in discord in its form and movement with the form and movement of nature, produces a sterile movement which gives no birth to future movements, but dies as it is made. (Duncan, 1983)

She sought first principles, the origin of movement, and found in her solar plexus the impulse which generates all possibilities. With this knowledge, she asserted that movement had only to be rediscovered rather than invented. Nature was, for her, a rationale for all things. In life as well as art she believed in freedom and expressivity, challenging the traditional not only in dance but in sexual mores, in the restrictive clothing of the time, and in women's roles. Her own was the first naked foot seen on the Western stage in 1600 years (de Mille, 1980, p. 45).

Though she spent most of her career in Europe, Duncan described her dance as having sprung from America, from a democratic society with a free point of view (de Mille, 1980, p. 44). Americans, she thought, should only be satisfied with their own ideal of beauty rather than accepting the aesthetic values of other cultures and times, and she was perhaps the first to say so:

> I see America dancing, beautiful, strong ... with great strides, leaps and bounds, with lifted forehead and far-spread arms, dancing the language of our pioneers, the fortitude of our heroes, the justice, kindness, purity of our women, and through it all the inspired love and tenderness of our mothers. When the American children dance this way, it will make of them Beautiful Beings worthy of the name Democracy. (Ruyter, p. 46)

Duncan was akin to literary romantics of the mid-1800s in looking to nature for authenticity, and she gained her perspective from the era's concern for humanity in an increasingly mechanized world (Ruyter, p. 50). A major part of her legacy lies in the questions she raised: Are we meant to move in unnatural ways? Can a distortion of nature be equated with beauty? From whence does all movement spring? Before her time, dancing was meant to be pleasant, innocuous, and lively (Terry,

1971, p. 50). Through her writings, her associations, and her performance, Duncan set it on a level with the other arts. While little of her actual work has survived, her ideas have prevailed: Her search for the genesis of movement, her use of dance for political and social statements, and her thoughts on breaking down the barriers between audience and performer have made her a model for modern dancers at least through the 1960s. Some of her ideas were thirty to forty years ahead of their time, only coming to fruition in the late 1950s when happenings began to merge the audience with the art, and in the 1960s with the work of the Judson Dance Theater.

From Duncan, we inherit the point of view that it is possible to conceptualize and analyze dance philosophically, politically, aesthetically, and morally. As important as she was, however, the chances are good that some form of modern dance would have developed without her, due to the work of Ruth St. Denis and Ted Shawn. St. Denis's legacy can, in fact, be more concretely felt here than Duncan's because St. Denis did most of her work in the United States. If Duncan's impact stemmed from her life and her ideas, St. Denis's influence manifests itself in the careers of her students and in the development of a teaching method. Both created their own paths, since at the time there were few options for the young woman with aspirations to be both artist and dancer. Opportunities in dance were limited to performing in ballet or vaudeville, and there were no standards by which to judge work like theirs, no rules for them to follow.

St. Denis created dances which attempted to unify soul and body, and to speak to the profundity of Eastern thought. She developed a movement vocabulary and costumes suited to her themes and, like Duncan, approached her performances as an artist rather than an entertainer. She is believed to be the first American dancer to appear in a full-length dance performance (Terry, p. 52). Walter Terry quotes St. Denis:

> Don't ask me why it had to be a new dance form that I should create instead of drama or poetry or painting. I don't know. At that time there was no dance form I could follow. I was born into a world of splits and kicks in vaudeville and a completely moribund ballet at the opera. No food there for my voracious appetite. (p. 57)

St. Denis married Ted Shawn, a young American dancer, in 1914. Together they founded Denishawn, a school and company which, during the fifteen years of its existence (1915–1930), provided a training ground for the next revolution. While Miss Ruth, as she was called, was at heart a performer, Shawn was an educator and proselytizer as well as an artist. The school reflected his belief that training in a wide variety of styles was the best way to create a wholeness in dance, which could then be metamorphosed into a personal style of expression. Denishawn was very successful, attracting students of education and serious purpose, among them, Martha Graham, Doris Humphrey, and Charles Weidman. For the first time in America, young women from good families studied dance professionally and men became interested in dance beyond ballroom and tap. It was the only school in the country offering a complete program of dance study. There were classes in freestyle (barefoot) ballet and ethnic dance, lectures on dance history, philosophy of movement, Oriental art, and courses in music, lighting, make-up, and other related areas (Stodelle, 1984, p. 22). This approach to dance education, developing the mind along with the body, was revolutionary in America in 1915.

The school supported the company, which toured nationally and internationally with a repertoire based on Oriental and other ethnic themes. On tour, the dancers were paid a salary, out of which they had to pay for their own train tickets and lodging. Not only was the Denishawn company serious about art, bringing dance to many American cities and towns which had never seen anything like it before, but it also toured the vaudeville circuit, using the commercial stage as a means of making money to support its artistic enterprises. This was seen as a necessity by Shawn and St. Denis, but the conflicting goals of art and entertainment produced division within the company and later become one of the reasons why Humphrey and Weidman left Denishawn (Humphrey, 1966).

The Early Moderns

Doris Humphrey came to Denishawn, already a trained dancer, in 1917, one year after Graham had come as a twenty-two year old beginner. The latter was Shawn's student, and later his protege, while Humphrey performed with the Ruth St. Denis Concert Dancers (Stodelle, 1984, p. 30). The two worked together only once, performing on the same program, though not in the same dances, just before Graham left the company in 1923. Humphrey stayed another five years and left in 1928.

Rivals in most ways, these two were alike in feeling that America required its own form of dance, with roots in the present time. Each experimented with ways of moving which for her expressed the truth of humankind, the contradictions of love, fear, hostility, and beauty. Over time, Graham developed a technique out of her own body feelings, building a study of breath into contraction and release, and allowing that to carry her into powerful, emotion-packed movement. Humphrey, on the other hand, sought the laws of the universe, experimenting with gravity and the still point in order to devise movement based on fall and recovery, danger and peace. "Moving the body stirs the emotions," she wrote, while Graham described her process in almost opposite terms: "Out of emotion comes form" (Stodelle, 1984, p. 62).

Working separately, these two evolved differing aspects of a dance unlike any seen to that time: strong, earthy, percussive, uncompromising, unadorned. Eleanor King, who performed with Humphrey from 1928 to 1935, writes that "Their goals were similar, but their natures—mother Martha and Doric Doris, as Louis Horst put it—and their works were as different as night and day" (1978, p. 51). Writing about their work in 1933, John Martin, dance critic for the *New York Times*, characterized the modern dance as a point of view. It was dance created not for technical display as is ballet, he said, or for self-expression, as in the interpretive dance current at the time, but to "externalize authentic, personal experience" (Cohen, 1966, p. 4).

For Denishawn and Duncan, dance had been truth and spirituality, and the beauty of natural being. With the 1930s came a time of economic depression, difficult living conditions at home, and a troubling political situation abroad. These years required acknowledgment of a greater reality, one which included fear and desperation, and dance artists responded with an art which sought to reveal the significant by eliminating the decorative, superficial, and glib. This new dance was consciously revolutionary, much of it devoted to the human struggle, to social issues, and politics. Graham's stated aim was "to make apparent once again the inner realities behind the accepted symbols" (Cohen, p. 7). Humphrey declared, "My dance is concerned with immediate, human values" (Stodelle, 1978, p. 17).

The work was extreme, without decorative elements. Costumes, lighting, and decor were purely functional, in keeping with the economic situation throughout the country and the rigorous intent of the artists.

Though the field was divided into companies or camps, all were united, dancers and choreographers alike, in struggling to legitimize the new form. Each concert combined the excitement of anticipation and possibility with the fervor of fighting for an aesthetic cause. Martin, at the *Times*, championed the work, but the concert-going public was often shocked and confused.

During these years, dancing was an exciting and fervent way of life marked by poverty. According to Hyla Rubin Samroch, who danced with Humphrey in the early 1930s,

> Doris demanded the most from her "girls", expected it was all right for them to starve for their art. Unless you had an outside job (which you were expected to relinquish anytime out of town engagements or tours came along) or you had someone rich to house and feed you . . . you could not survive the rigors of the dance field. (King, 1978, p. 305)

Ernestine Stodelle, another dancer with the Doris Humphrey and Charles Weidman Concert Group during that period, describes life as a member of the company and notes the sense of mission they shared despite hardship:

> Performances were very infrequent, and they paid a mere ten dollars apiece. But in those Depression times even a teaching job was hard to come by. . . . Some of the Group members existed by posing for artists and sculptors (at one dollar per hour), and a few were waitresses in small downtown restaurants. We had to settle for part-time work; rehearsals were in the evenings, and, occasionally, costume fittings or special assignments occurred during the day. And there were other, more subtle responsibilities, voluntarily assumed: reading books of philosophy and poetry; being conversant with contemporary literature; going to music concerts and art museums. Self-cultivation was a part of the process of growing into a truly distinctive modern dancer; that was understood from the beginning. (1978, p. 7)

Agnes de Mille, herself a young dancer in the 1930s, writes a nearly parallel description of the Graham company at that time:

> The girls worked for nothing, of course. The box office barely paid the advertising and rental, never any of the rehearsal costs. Martha taught the year round to pay these and her living. To meet their expenses, some of her pupils waited on table. None of them were adequately fed or housed.

These girls were not to be thought of as the usual illiterate student who fills the ballet schools. They were all adults; many held degrees of one sort or another and had deliberately chosen this form of dancing as opposed to the traditional for serious and lasting reasons. (1952, p. 156)

The deep commitment felt by modern dancers during those early years was almost religious; the dedication, absolute.

Like vestal virgins, modern dancers were committed to one master. If you were a disciple of one artist, you could not study with another. Graham dancers were even restrained from attending performances of other modern artists, lest the purity of their vision become clouded. (King, p. 47)

As the field developed throughout the 1930s, dance artists hoped to unionize and gain a living wage. Slowly, however, it became clear that individualism and social relevance, which were keystones of the new aesthetic, would not draw the general audience in large enough numbers to avoid seasonal financial deficits. Modern dance gained respect and attention as an art during the decade, but the income it generated would not, on the whole, support a union pay scale (Wheeler, 1986). Nevertheless, work continued. According to Don McDonagh, Graham

... simply refused to consider money in any serious relation to what she was doing. Her attitude was that, if one devoted oneself to modern dance for the money, then one was in it for the wrong reasons. She gave her dancers whatever payment she could when she could, but she relied on personal loyalty, not a paycheck, as the cement to keep her organization together. To discuss money was to betray art, and later in her career, when substantial sums were available for her company, she still refused to consider money of any importance. Her simple view was: Crusaders don't expect paychecks. (1973, p. 88)

Nevertheless, after a decade of striving, the 1940s brought a more relaxed atmosphere in modern dance, a time of assimilation, building on what had been achieved. As King notes, the early moderns had completely rejected ballet and all that it implied, but

... after the first flush of puritanical independence from all elements of tainted theatricality, the crusaders a decade later relaxed their aversion to ballet barres, and basic classical discipline slowly crept into the once revolutionary studios. (p. 82)

As the concert-going public grew more receptive to the new dance, energy could be put to refining techniques and expanding theatricality and thematic range. Gradually, decoration and elaboration crept into the form.

A Period of Consolidation

During the 1940s and much of the 1950s, Humphrey, Weidman, Graham, and the German-born Hanya Holm were the acknowledged giants in the field and all worked in New York. At this time, the circle of masters was closed and rarely opened to accept younger artists. It was a period of consolidation. Sally Banes (1987) writes that during these years, modern dance was concerned with production values and a theatrical product. While the new dance was being accepted, it was losing its potency, as well as the ability to shock and bring to awareness. Moreover, with its appeal to the intelligentsia, it was now becoming even more esoteric than the ballet.

The form, during this period, was stable as was the structure of the field, and the life of a dancer was still that of a disciple. In conversation, Dorothy Berea Silver, a member of the Graham company from 1946–1949 describes relations within the company as like a family:

> ...we were siblings.... She [Graham] wanted to know everything about [you], wanted to have a lot of control...we were pieces of her work....She wanted to make sure we had certain experiences....She had us all take a poetry course....All of my experience was funneled into dance—my life—everything about it was in reference to dance....None of it was a job....You could not really survive the kind of work we were doing unless you really believed in her work—the standards, the expectations, the hours, dancing and waiting. (personal communication, May 1988)

The Graham company was (and still is) one of the few union groups (American Guild of Musical Artists). In those days, this meant that dancers were paid for performances and for two weeks of rehearsal before each yearly New York season. Tours were salaried, but there was no housing allowance as there is today, and dancers paid for their own rooms, which were booked by the company. When not on tour, performers survived by teaching or demonstrating at the Graham Studio, modeling, or dancing at places like the Roxy. Also, at this time, though

Graham had priority, nearly all the dancers performed with other groups when she was not in rehearsal. Silver danced with Merce Cunningham and Nina Fonaroff, both of whom were non-union and so paid only for performances.

Finances were, as always, difficult. "There were not grants," Silver recalls, "and I don't think anyone thought they deserved a grant. . . . My attitude was, why should anyone give us money? Let us perform, and then you pay. . . ." The concept of the grant had yet to be developed. Choreographers depended heavily on private patronage and volunteers. Graham had patrons, but still endured severe financial difficulties. She declared bankruptcy during the late 1940s. Silver describes Graham as "like the rest of us," supporting herself with teaching and some commissions. The Graham values were clear, however: "Whatever she wanted to have for her pieces, she really got. She just would not go second class on costumes and a lot of things like that." If times were hard, and the union had decreed a certain pay scale, Graham "would sometimes ask us to make a financial adjustment." Asked how the company responded to these requests, Silver replied:

> When it came to the art and the single artist, it wasn't like the Teamsters—you were employed by this artist and were dependent on whether she used you. How many jobs dancing were there? . . . You were lucky to be working at dancing. . . . We understood Martha's point of view toward her art. We were part of her art. We had faith in Martha's aesthetic. (1988)

Devotion to the form, sacrifice, a sense of family, hierarchical relations, and the mystique of genius all characterize the dance field during the 1940s. De Mille describes young dancers of the time coming to choreographers

> . . . the way apprentices come to great painters. The new technique, the style, the compositions were worked out together, master and pupil struggling with the same problems. The performers . . . gave their whole time, their strength, and their youth to the formation of the techniques . . . asking merely to serve the art form and their chosen master. . . . The modern dancer of the 1930s and 1940s was in point of view less like a ballet dancer . . . than like an acolyte, or a Renaissance craftsman. (1980, p. 110)

As the 1940s gave way to the 1950s, these company dancers matured, and many began choreographic careers of their own—Jose Limon, Anna Sokolow, Merce Cunningham, Erick Hawkins, and Alwin Nikolais outstanding among them. The field had gained a certain respectability, and in the process, shed its rough edges, developing codified techniques and stylized vocabularies. That process of refinement went on throughout the 1950s. Choreographers continued to base their dances on musical forms and literary themes, using movement as a means of expression. Performances were given in proscenium theaters; theatrical lighting, costumes, and decor were used to create illusion, and predictably, some performers became stars, bigger than life, within the dance world. It was the Eisenhower period in the United States, a time of calm and peace, economic well-being, and family-centered life. At this point, modern dance was a thoroughly theatrical form.

Another radical shift was in the making, however. Merce Cunningham, formerly a dancer with Graham, had, for some years, been collaborating with composer John Cage, making dances which de-emphasized expression. His work broke with "traditional" modern dance in two important ways: he assimilated ballet's verticality and legwork into the vocabulary, and he brought movement to the fore, making it an end in itself. Though he retained a technical, dancerly style, his experiments with chance elements and indeterminacy effectively separated the artist's will from the art, and removed the interdependency of music, decor, and dance. Most important in his revolutionary work was the rejection of traditional definitions of communication and meaning.

Former Graham dancer Silver views these innovations as a reaction to Graham, who used dancers as factors of her own expression. Cunningham's work was not about anything but dancing; it intended no meaning beyond what actually was presented, told no story and followed no music. As a choreographer, he refused to direct the audience's eye through the manipulation of space and time, allowing the viewer to make selections among the dancers on stage and, essentially, to create an individual version of his work, according to the choices made.

The modern dance world was suspicious, even hostile. In the early years, John Martin, still at the *New York Times*, refused to review Cunningham's concerts, effectively withholding both credibility and visibility among the general public. The underground channels, however, were open, and the New York art world sensed that something important was about to happen.

The Judson Revolution

Cunningham's work and that of his collaborator, John Cage, served as a springboard into a reconception which would deeply affect the course of the field. At the end of the 1950s, there was a general sense around the Cunningham-Cage camp that modern dance had lost the vitality it once had had. In response, Cage invited Robert Dunn to conduct a choreography workshop at the Cunningham studio. At the time, Louis Horst and Doris Humphrey were the major influences in dance composition, and some felt their classes were too structured for real exploration. Horst, a composer, built his classes around musical forms, while Humphrey worked with dance in theatrical terms. Dunn, also a composer and an accompanist at the Cunningham studio, offered an alternative to their ideas by teaching the musical structures of composers like Cage and Pierre Boulez, not as musical forms, but as time constructs. His class worked with concepts of chance, noise, indeterminacy, and silence. Assignments were deliberately loose and many choices were left to the students.

During the first year, the group included Yvonne Rainer, Steve Paxton, and Simone Forti. They met once a week and focused on working with energy, repetition, juxtaposition, and stillness. Dunn's method was to analyze rather than criticize, to discuss what was seen, and finally to ask what had been intended. Forti, who had come to New York after studying with Ann Halprin in California, stayed with the workshop for the first year. She describes her experience as follows:

> The one teacher I connected with in New York was Bob Dunn. He was teaching a composition class at the Merce Cunningham studio in the fall of 1960. Dunn began the course by introducing us to John Cage's scores....
> The Cage scores got the class off to a good start. They provided us with a clear point of departure, and performing them had the effect of helping us bypass inhibitions on making pieces. We started producing a lot of material, and, once we were rolling, we had something to learn from. Especially towards the beginning of the course, Dunn urged us to work on our own pieces quickly, without suffering over them. And throughout the course he urged us to be clearly aware of the methods we were using in working, whatever they might be. (1974, p. 36)

Yvonne Rainer had begun studying dance earnestly in 1959 at the age of twenty-five. She was an active force in Dunn's workshop from the beginning and stayed with it from 1960–1964 as it evolved into the Judson Dance Theater. Here, she reflects on the philosophical position which the workshop, once going, had begun to assume:

> Bob . . . was happy to see so much activity loosed by whatever means. He seemed as interested in how something was presented as by what method it was made. And, of course, the Cagean idea that chance offered an alternative to the masterpiece was operating very strongly. In retrospect this must have secretly galled me, as I continue (secretly) to aspire to making masterpieces. (1974, p. 7)

By 1962, after two years of studio work, the class had expanded to include more dancers and a number of composers and visual artists. It was an artistic community in a real sense and provided a rich exchange. Feeling ready for public response at this point, but without funds, they arranged to produce a concert of work at Judson Church in Greenwich Village. The audience was composed largely of friends and artists. According to Rainer:

> That first concert of dance turned out to be a three-hour marathon for a capacity audience of about 300 sitting from beginning to end in the un-air conditioned 90 degree heat. The selection of the program had been hammered out . . . with Bob Dunn as the cool-headed prow of a sometimes overheated ship. He was responsible for the organization of the program. (1974, p. 8)

Dunn's attitude toward performance and choreography ran distinctly counter to tradition and preciousness, and brought into question the common conception of concert order. Dances were presented simultaneously, overlapping, broken up, used as sequences and overtures, and performed during intermission (Banes, 1983). Overall, the Judson concerts were as experimental as the work they presented, avoiding a traditional climax, often beginning and ending with solos. The first performance set the course for the next few years. Rainer writes:

> We were all wildly ecstatic afterwards, and with good reason. Aside from the enthusiasm of the audience, the church seemed a positive alternative to the once-a-year hire-a-hall mode of operating that had plagued the struggling modern dancer before. Here we could present things more frequently, more informally, and more cheaply, and—most important of all—

more cooperatively. If I thought that much of what went on in the workshop was a bunch of nonsense, I also had a dread of isolation, which made me place great value on being part of a group. (1974, p. 8)

This was the beginning of a series of concerts which expanded the boundaries of modern dance so violently that the term "postmodern" came into use to describe the work being shown.

Many of the values and attitudes brought to the fore at Judson were shaped by the 1960s. It was an era of pacifism and civil rights, blending high regard for human life with the powerful feeling that all things could be changed. Culture-wide, there was experimentation with sex, drugs, and lifestyle. In the art world there was concern for the reinvention of American culture and a rejection of the managerial values which dominate our economic system (Gans, 1974, p. 98). The visual arts saw a period of rapid change. Abstract expressionism was becoming popular with the public and in response, high art moved off into the realms of pop, op, photographic realism, minimal, and conceptual art in quick succession (Gans, p. 81). The Judson choreographers were carried along on this social and artistic journey.

Like pop artists, they were fascinated by the ordinary, and included everyday objects and activities in their dances, giving them a context that made the commonplace strange and new again (Banes, 1983, p. 105). The found gesture, either from daily life or commercial dance, was used in much the same way that the found object—junk, the imagery of commercial art, or industrial products—was used in the visual arts. Just as Pop Art was a reaction to Abstract Expressionism, the new, postmodern dance challenged both the personal expressionism and the abstract gestures of the older generation of modern dancers. Ballet and dance "steps" became just another resource, along with pedestrian and sports movements, and stillness, talking, and games. This effectively raised the point that the material which goes into a dance may not be the criterion which distinguishes it as a work of art. Chance methods, collage, and indeterminacy were all seen as ways to free oneself from one's own limitations. As Rainer explained, "The chance operation is useful when one is in a quandary, is in a stalemate with one's body, is immobilized by habits no longer useful, is in need of clues to new images...." (Banes, 1983, p. 78).

Free association, cooperative choice-making, slow meditation, lists, handling objects, and solving tasks were other methods used to change the focus of both choreographers and performers, facilitating invention and breaking the hold of tradition. The interest in real time and energy (as opposed to the choreographer's usual manipulation of time, the customary stretch and lift of the dancer's body) evoked a human scale and an intimacy which modern dance had once had, but lost in its fascination with theatricality (Banes, 1983, p. 10).

The invention of new forms and structuring devices was one focus of the Judson group. Another was in maintaining a wide range of options. They accomplished this partly through the avoidance of codified technique, viewed, by them, as a limiting factor in the work of the previous generation. This was a political decision as well; a standard, stylized way of moving was seen as creating an inequality among performers and a barrier between performer and audience. The Judson choreographers aimed to make art without the persona of the artist, to dispel theatrical illusion, and to foreground the medium rather than the meaning. Their dances were informal, intimate, pedestrian, and low key, costumed in street clothes or leotards, and performed in open spaces. They tried not to be dancerly, but to connect dance with life and be natural, and so allowed the untrained, nondance movement of the composers and visual artists in the workshop to influence the group aesthetic. In an effort to be rid of the usual, seductive involvement with the audience, they consciously did away with performing and aimed at simply doing (Hanna, 1987a, p. 23).

Along with seeking to separate dance from a dependence on idealized, stylized movements, the Judson choreographers were concerned, as Cunningham was, with wanting to free dance from the literary base it had developed and to make it independent of musical forms. They, too, refused to give in to the accepted requirements of "communication" and "meaning," and so brought into question basic materials and traditions of dance (Banes, 1983, p. 40). With movement which was natural and pedestrian, task-oriented, and simply performed, their dances presented a new kind of viewing experience. Rainer writes about her work:

> When I talk about connections and meaning, I'm talking about the emotional load of a particular event and not about what it signifies. Its signification is always very clear. I don't deal with symbols, I deal with categories of things and they have varying degrees of emotional load. (1974, p. 108)

Rather than a means to expression or technical display, dance had come to be about motion and structure. Without overtly expressive or illusionistic effects, or references beyond itself, movement was exposed and made meaningful, revealing details of life and humanness. Traditional sources of meaning were removed, and the dance itself became visible.

In Dunn's workshop, aesthetics and politics had been thoroughly blended. The first two years of concerts (1962–1964) were cooperative and voluntary with a nondiscriminatory policy regarding works performed and workshop participation. Efforts to consolidate or institutionalize the group which we now know as the Judson Dance Theater were resisted, creating a fluidity in energy and membership. Members rejected the hierarchy typical of dance companies and made all important decisions by consensus.

In the philosophical impulses behind this work, modern dancers once again found a deep meaning in their art, a humanism, and a connection to democratic values. The ideas which gave rise to the Judson period brought new significance and function to the art and became the hallmark of postmodern choreography until the late 1970s. Not only were the structure and content of dances changed, and new meaning given to process in choreography, but Judson affected the social institution of dance viewing as well. Through the pragmatic and economic decision to perform in a church, the group was instrumental in developing the use of alternate spaces for showing dances, creating a tradition for postmodern dance and setting the scene for the development of untold numbers of small companies and independent choreographers in the years ahead. Additionally, the practice of giving concerts during the hot New York summer has permanently expanded the dance season.

In 1961, coincidentally with Judson, John Martin commented in the *Times* that, for the first time, the bulk of the New York season was produced by male choreographers (Hanna, 1987b, p. 39). This shift marked the growing acceptability of the field, even if, economically, the situation for dancers had not changed. Although the rise of humanistic values in the 1960s served to demystify the master artist of early days, dancers maintained a devotion to the art, a sense of calling, and, for the most part, expected to teach or work at odd jobs in order to continue dancing and choreographing. Paul Taylor, a former dancer with Graham, illustrates this with a remark that in 1961, his company was rehearsing late into the night: "Like Martha's, my dancers are committed to their work and are rehearsing for free; in modern dance at this time, paid rehearsals are pretty much unheard of" (Taylor, 1987, p. 122).

Paradoxically, it was the possibility of making money with their art which eroded the unity of the Judson Dance Theater and contributed to the dissolution of the original group (Banes, 1983). Growing notoriety brought offers of paid performances to the most visible in that group, and a schism was formed. As long as no one had been paid, the lack of money was not a problem; with the possibility of remuneration, a new kind of hierarchy arose. Competition and division replaced consensus and Judson slowly dissolved.

Though the late 1960s and the 1970s were years of burgeoning growth and expansion throughout the field in terms of sheer numbers, artistically, they were like the 1940s and 1950s, years of consolidation. Performances centered largely in loft spaces, churches, and art galleries, in line with the postmodern aesthetic. According to Banes, there were two major choreographic thrusts in the 1970s. The first maintained a distance from expression, combining an almost scientific or mathematical approach to movement with low key presentation. The aesthetic, which Banes connects to a post-Watergate and oil crisis mentality, seemed to be one of baring the facts and conserving the means. The second thrust derived from Eastern thought and was involved with metaphysical, spiritual, or mythic values. It used theatrical elements in addition to structural devices such as radical juxtaposition and repetition, and so combined expression with postmodernism. Once again, symbols and ideas put forward in revolution were being assimilated into the culture and losing their strength along with their stridency.

Dancing in the 1980s

Though the Judson point of view continues to inform much of today's work, we have lately sought a more traditional sense of order in our dance. The 1980s saw a return to virtuosity as a high value, along with elegance and adornment in both movement and costuming. This is explained, perhaps, by American culture which, during this period, had more to do with immediate pleasure and consumerism and less with ideas. If the 1960s and 1970s were content to let dance simply "be" instead of "mean," the 1980s required a high impact, more substantive form, glossy, attractive, pointing the way to order in a chaotic world. Technique became increasingly important.

In New York City, many professional modern dancers take a daily ballet class, making that the main thrust of their training. It is assumed that the rigors of ballet will prepare the dancer for anything a modern dance choreographer might require. There is another, more subtle result of this kind of training, however. Ballet is a style which attempts to deny gravity and mask effort, so the weight and visible energy with which the early moderns worked are lost. Moreover, because ballet training is designed to fit dancers to a standard, perfect form, it strips them of their uniqueness: as they work for perfection, they work against their own individuality. This is happening across the field, diminishing the differences between company styles and erasing the divergent approaches which we saw with early Graham and Humphrey. Modern dance now has a more uniformly—if more brilliantly—trained pool of dancers available for work, many of whom resemble barefoot ballet dancers.

In choreography, expression is seeing a return, as are character, mood, and relationship, though sometimes in such a way as to resist definitive interpretation. Narrative is reappearing, now often as a verbal text accompanying abstract movement. This work does not attempt the seamless theatrical illusion of Graham and Humphrey. Media, music, and effects are used to enhance and emphasize, making work accessible on a number of levels. The form seems to be building on the consolidation of the 1970s, while letting the culture lead the art. The music scene now provides the context for much dance, rather than the visual arts, as was the case in the 1960s. In New York and elsewhere, works are shown at cabarets, discos, and clubs, forming ties with popular music and seemingly pointing dance away from the realm of high art and toward the entertainment industry.

Choreography is involved with energy and cleverness, with feats of endurance and skill, and hard-hitting physicality. From the concern with form which Judson introduced, the balletic demands of Cunningham, and a mastery of special effects technology, an art has emerged which exists on the surface and places its emphasis on the visible and the kinesthetic. Sally Banes sees this development as a political expression, an anti-elitist point of view which makes the art available to a wide-ranging audience (1987, p. xxxv).

The aim for a more general accessibility, however, might also be seen in terms of economics. Moreover, it can be argued that economic influence goes beyond aesthetics into the very structure of the field, influencing dance training, the standards of success, the structure of dance organizations, and the lifestyle of dancers. The profession is shaped by an interest in technical excellence, in preserving repertory and maintaining permanent, stable companies, all, most likely, a response to the economic demands of touring, funding sources, and producers (Banes, 1987, p. xxvii). In fact, economics seems to be the dominant value system in dance, determining what is done, how to train for it, who will do it, and how it will be produced.

The conflicting pulls of entertainment and art have presented an increasingly difficult choice for dance artists. Sometimes it has been a choice between the competing values of commercial and critical success, sometimes between popularity and authenticity. Throughout most of this century, modern dancers have held to revolutionary ideals, breaking new ground in spite of financial risk and the lack of acceptance inevitably associated with such work. This goal and the deliberate appropriation of marginal positions have given the form its distinct point of view toward the function of art. In his or her way each seminal dance artist has been an educator, teaching what dance can be, leading audiences into new directions and new ways of conceiving dance, art, and life. Their work has given modern dance a heritage which prizes exploration as a process and art as an experience, and a tradition which values integrity, individualism and social relevance beyond commercial success. Choreography designed to display ego or attract the crowds has, in fact, historically been held to be philosophically at odds with the modern dance ethic (Cohen, 1966, p. 13).

Modern dance in the late 1980s, however, has found it extremely difficult to maintain its vision, a reality which can best be examined from the perspective of what has been called postmodern thought.[1] "Postmodern thought" is a highly complex concept, elusive in meaning, which can perhaps be generally characterized as a mode of existence where involvement with image and selling dominates, and depth has been replaced with such surface values as packaging and name-recognition.

Fredric Jameson (1984) is one of the more influential commentators and interpreters of postmodern thought. He describes the postmodern world as a vast world-market culture without local boundaries and landmarks, all-enveloping, making the marginal toe-hold a present-day impossibility. He speaks of being submerged in "the new space of postmodernism," which is equated with "the world of late capitalism." The postmodern aesthetic is characterized as a market aesthetic. According

---

[1]Although dance writers have used the term "postmodern" in connection with the Judson Dance Theater and the work that followed, it was not until the 1980s that modern dance artists have actually adopted the aesthetic concerns associated with that term in other art forms.

to Jameson, art today is disarmed and reabsorbed by the large scale commercial culture, and so has lost the critical distance necessary to cultural resistance. If all art is for sale, there can be no marginal positions.

Furthermore, in correlating postmodernism with the development of multinational capitalism, Jameson gives the phenomenon a historical dimension and thus a reality with which we can identify as we strive to cope (1984, p. 85). The culture has evolved faster than our capabilities and we, artists and nonartists alike, have been swept along, unable to gain our bearings. It remains for the art of the future to find a means of comprehending the vastness of the new world space, Jameson says, to aid us all in positioning ourselves within it, both personally and collectively, so that we may regain the means to struggle and act.

If culture is now being defined in terms of "markets" then the issue of financial support for dance becomes at once significant and problematic. Since the time frame for the gradual change in dynamics within modern dance after Judson roughly parallels the development of funding procedures institutionalized in the 1960s, and simultaneously, the beginning of a large new market for American modern dance stimulated by the National Endowment for the Arts, Jameson's is an intriguing theory for the field. The developing commercial culture created a vacuum, a worldwide market with which the loosely organized field of modern dancers could not easily cope. An organizing force was needed, a means of bringing dance into that market. With the founding of the Endowment in 1965, just at the end of the Judson era, the field acquired such a force, which set about shaping the profession organizationally, geographically, economically, and not incidentally, aesthetically.

Over the past twenty years, modern dance as a field has experienced profound, and perhaps irreversible, changes in conjunction with the policies instituted by funding agencies and the mode of thinking which has come about by learning to describe artistic process in economic terms. Through efforts to enhance the quality of the art, to make it accessible to the public and give it the grounds for financial security, what seems an inversion of the modern dance vision and priorities has occurred. Where marketing and funding considerations used to be peripheral, logistical concerns, they now bear on central, artistic choices. This colors all aspects of the field, from the relationship between cast and choreographer, to the role of a company within its community, to the emphasis within a company repertory. And not least, it has had profound effect on the way in which the field prepares young dancers.

Judson marked the last major period of reconception in the field, the last time when choreography was actively concerned with the creation of new symbols (Rainer's claim that she does not work with symbols notwithstanding). A possible interpretation of this lag might be the commonly cited theory of thirty year cycles: we had Duncan and St. Denis at the turn of the century, Graham and Humphrey in the 1930s, Judson in the 1960s, and now we are simply in another period of consolidation, awaiting the next creative revolution. Arthur Schlesinger, Jr. was recently quoted in the *Greensboro News and Record*, citing this phenomenon in reference to politics: "If the rhythm of politics holds true, the 1990s in the United States will be much more like the 1960s" (1988, p. A3). If Jameson is right, however, we have entered a new period of history, and the changes we have seen can be attributed to essential shifts in our model of the world. These have occurred so slowly that we have not been attuned to them, perhaps not even noticed that the values we once held important are no longer guiding the course.

Liz Lerman

Bill T. Jones

Twyla Tharp

The National Endowment for the Arts and Its Impact on Modern Dance

Introduction

Throughout its brief history, and particularly at the beginning, the National Endowment for the Arts has played a dynamic role in reshaping the art world by means of distributing funds and through its influence, not only on other government funding agencies but on foundations and corporations as well. In terms of dance, the relatively sudden availability of money brought about by Endowment policies deeply affected the organization of the professional field and so, also, the lives of artists and their work. Other agencies have been important too, most notably, the Ford Foundation, which has had a strong impact on the finances of ballet companies and their schools.

For modern dance, however, it is widely accepted that the major funding influence has been the NEA. Its subsidy of sponsoring organizations, either directly or through state arts councils, its promotion of touring and management, and the catalytic effect it has had on other funding agencies, have all had profound influence on the development and visibility of modern dance nationwide. The field has gradually become decentralized, touring has become a way of life for modern dance companies, and not-for-profit corporate status has become the organizational model across the field, with community-based boards of directors and professional management the rule.

Prior to the founding of the National Endowment for the Arts in 1965, the United States relied heavily on volunteerism and private initiative and patronage for the support of the arts. Since the New Deal, there had been little federal government involvement in arts funding. Before 1967, when the NEA began making block grants to state arts councils, twenty-two states, fewer than half, had appropriated any funds to a state arts agency. The combined appropriations for the twenty-one states other than New York was $505,000 at that time, barely enough to pay the salary of a single full-time staff member in each state. By 1972, however, all fifty states and the District of Columbia, Puerto Rico, and three overseas jurisdictions had arts council receiving both NEA money and state appropriations. Most of these councils were formed, not from an autonomous swelling of interest in the arts at the state level, but as a direct result of the availability of NEA funds for the purpose (Netzer, 1978, p. 90).

The literature is not clear about the first post-New Deal attempts at a national arts policy. Harlen E. Hoffa mentions being part of the Arts and Humanities Program of the Office of Education in 1965, "the only arts presence in the panoply of federal programs. . . . Our activities were limited to supporting educational research" (1981, p. 4). W. McNeil Lowry, on the other hand, discusses indirect federal help for arts institutions through the underwriting of portions of their audiences, as a result of the 1965 Titles I and III of the amended National Defense Education Act administered by the Department of Health, Education and Welfare (1978, p. 17). Whatever the case, President Lyndon Johnson signed the legislation which finally established the twin Endowments of the Arts and Humanities in 1965. According to Lowry, Johnson had a personal interest in demonstrating support for cultural activities equal to or surpassing that of former president John F. Kennedy. This agenda, coupled with the fact that Johnson had the support of a large Democratic majority in the House of Representatives after the election of 1964, made the budget for the Great Society, including the Endowments, a reality (p. 18).

The legislation itself acknowledged the long-standing American tradition of private patronage, as it decreed

> that the encouragement and support of national progress and scholarship in the humanities and the arts, while primarily a matter for private and local initiative, is also an appropriate matter of concern to the Federal Government. (Hoffa, 1981, p. 5)

So stating, the Congress instituted the National Foundation of the Arts and Humanities. President Johnson signed it into law on September 29, 1965 with the following words:

> In the long history of man, countless empires and nations have come and gone. Those which created no lasting works of art are reduced to small footnotes in history's catalogue. Art is a nation's most precious heritage. For it is in our works of art that we reveal to ourselves, and to others, the inner vision which guides us as a nation. (National Endowment for the Arts, 1968, p. 5)

Ever since, policy and operations decisions have rested with the Endowment's administrative staff.

A statement of mission is spelled out in all NEA *Applications Guidelines* and *Annual Reports*. The 1987 *Annual Report* reads:

> The mission of the National Endowment for the Arts is:
> • to foster the excellence, diversity, and vitality of the arts in the United States and
> • to help broaden the availability and appreciation of such excellence, diversity, and vitality.
> In implementing its mission, the Endowment must exercise care to preserve and improve the environment in which the arts have flourished. It must not, under any circumstances, impose a single aesthetic standard or attempt to direct the artistic content. (p. 222)

Review of the Literature

There is, generally, a scarcity of serious analysis of the Endowment's policies and no in-depth studies of the relationship of federal funding to dance specifically. Researchers have noted that while observers remark on the tremendous growth in arts funding since 1965, the phenomenon has received little systematic study (Goody, 1984, p. 144), and that the Endowment itself has not been forthcoming on its policy actions and their results. In 1978 Dick Netzer wrote:

> Unless NEA places a high priority on rapid and substantial improvement of information on the arts and in its own reporting, it will continue to function in considerable ignorance of both the circumstances surrounding public subsidy and the consequences of its own activities. (1978, p. 177)

At just about that time, the NEA established a research budget which it has continued to support. In 1987, $431,000 was allotted for five actions in this area, including a Congressionally mandated, comprehensive "State of the Arts" report describing the arts in America. An additional $11,550 was allotted by the Dance Program for its chapter in that report. In spite of this, however, the focus of NEA research seems general and undelineated as to, and even within, disciplines. For example, in its *Five-Year Planning Document 1990–94*, the Endowment writes comprehensively, discussing problems and recent successes. Dance is presented as one field, rather than separated out according to style; ballet, modern, and ethnic mix together giving the NEA a perspective that is sweeping instead of specific. Moreover, the text does not distinguish between creative artists and performers, choreographers and dancers, or between employed and self-employed artists. These are distinctions which I believe are basic to understanding the range of experience and point of view within the field, closely interacting with such factors as educational level, income, professional goals, and world view. Generalization of this kind discounts the differences which make for rich cross-fertilization, and fails to address issues which do not concern the broad center of the field.

Additionally, in gathering budgetary information, the NEA employs what seems a flawed data base: namely the eighty-six dance companies which have consistently applied to the Endowment from Fiscal Year 1983 to Fiscal Year 1986 (*Five-Year Planning Document 1990–94*, p. 121). Likely, this sample only represents the eighty-six companies best oriented to the Endowment system, since they are the ones continuously making application. And because they continuously make application, these may be the eighty-six most financially successful dance companies in the United States, not a representative sample. Any companies who were not consistent in their applications, because of a discouraging grant history or perhaps because of management problems or internal disorganization, are left out, as are the independent artist and the artist-teacher. Additionally, scant differentiation is made between ballet, modern and ethnic companies and there are no budgetary distinctions. As of this writing, that is the extent of NEA budgetary information on the dance field.

According to these data, the average season was noted to be thirty-five weeks in FY86 and the average salary for a dancer, under $13,000 (for thirty-five weeks) (*Five-Year Planning Document 1990–94*, p. 121). These figures are not typical of the vast majority of small modern dance companies, most of which are not able to pay dancers a weekly wage. Many have long and active histories though they do not apply to the Endowment under the Dance Company category because they do not meet the financial and organizational requirements or they have little hope of competing successfully with the larger, more visible national groups. The Contemporary Dance Theater of Cincinnati, discussed in Chapter III, is one such company. Under the present data base, budgetary information from groups like this is not factored in.

Since its founding, the Endowment's appropriations have grown from $2.5 million in 1965 to $168 million in 1988, pacing a rapid rise in general arts funding during that period. The *Annual Reports*, which provide a history of NEA appropriations, along with lists of panels, descriptions of all grants awarded, and a yearly financial summary, give no information on the question of parity among and within programs, why one art form has had priority over another for funds. A review of the *Reports* shows that a number of these de facto priorities have shifted over the years, but no discussion of the thinking behind these changes is presented. Whether such choices are avowedly policy decisions or not, they have the effect of becoming so because, as Hoffa says, practice tends to become precedent and precedent, almost invariably, becomes the basis for policy decisions (p. 11).

Michael S. Joyce also raises this issue, saying that the question is whether

> ... policy is made explicit, open, and public, in which case it can be studied ... or whether ... policy is tacit or implied, in which case it is likely to be uncritically accepted and enforced without public debate and with little opportunity for evaluation or reform. ... (1984, p. 29)

The latter seems to be the case at the Endowment, perhaps explained by the struggle the agency has faced in justifying its very existence, creating a self-protective posture in many aspects of its operations. Joyce discusses the unexplained shifts in policy and draws the following conclusion:

> The implied or tacit cultural policy that we found to be the custom at both the National Endowments helped to explain, in our view, the presence of programs supported for political and social reasons rather than for artistic or scholarly reasons. (p. 29)

NEA Impact on the Organizational Structure of Companies

In spite of the fact that the NEA has not been explicit in its policies, it is possible to look at what has been done and come to some understanding of the goals which have governed these actions. Since 1965, the United States has experienced an expansion of performing arts institutions and companies with no precedent in any similar period in any country (Lowry, p. 4). According to W. MacNeil Lowry, this was brought about by a combination of institutional, economic, and programmatic strategies, chief among them, the increased use of the nonprofit tax-exempt corporation by directors, producers, and choreographers, the rise in the percentage of Americans with a college education, a national effort to improve and expand training and performing institutions (begun by the Ford Foundation in 1957), and the founding of the National Endowment of the Arts (p. 6).

The word "institutions" in the preceding paragraph is one key to understanding the impact of the NEA. Samuel Lipman (1986) thinks that, at heart, our cultural policy amounts to the promotion and support of institutions, the presenters (museums, orchestras, and dance, opera, and theater companies) and the organized advocates. An analysis of figures provided by the *Annual Reports* reveals support for this view. As Lowry writes, the objective means of discovering the NEA's impact lies in determining funding proportions and therefore, presumably, priorities (1978, p. 22). The proportions for 1987 and 1988 show a heavy emphasis on supporting organizations rather than individuals. Although NEA support for choreographers rose from 2.4% of the dance budget in 1980 to nearly 9% in 1987, support for dance organizations has been, on the whole, much more comprehensive. In 1987, when dance program funds were $8,723,750, $778,000 was divided among 110 individual choreographers, amounting to an average $7,072 per artist. In the same year, 62% of the funds went to dance companies: $5,431,900 was divided among 97 groups, making the average award to companies $55,999. The remaining 29% went to other grant categories—general services to the field, special projects, dance/film/video, and grants to dance presenters—themselves overwhelmingly comprised of organizations.

In 1988, the figures broke down in much the same way: $814,000 (still representing 9% of the total) was distributed among 97 individual choreographers, amounting to an average of $8,392 per artist, while 58% of the $8,852,000 budget went to dance companies, and 33% to the remaining categories.

These figures would seem to make clear the Endowment's priorities and the way in which it has tried to shape the profession. However, Jack R. Lemmon, Dance Program administrator at the NEA, characterized the recent increases in Choreographer's Fellowships as an equally important reflection of the NEA's current attitude. The agency does not want to push people to institutionalize, he says, and so wants to be sure to provide support for individual artists. In Lemmon's opinion, the NEA is at its best when it is reactive rather than proactive. "We don't want to push people to *do* anything," he said (his emphasis) (personal communication, October 20, 1988). Nevertheless, as a means of promoting financial stability, federal policy has mandated that nonprofit, tax-exempt corporate status be in place before an organization is eligible for most NEA grants. As it became clear that this was the case, dance companies nationwide adopted that structure, writing bylaws, forming boards of directors, and organizing themselves as corporate institutions.

Before this push to organize companies, the dance field had been a loose aggregate of choreographic artists working independently, the most impoverished of American art forms (Baumol and Bowen, 1966, p. 31). William J. Baumol and William G. Bowen, writing in 1966, describe the situation in the field at that time:

> Typically a modern dance organization is administered in all its aspects by a single person—the choreographer. He either serves as his own secretary, accountant, and business manager or entrusts these tasks to a wife or friend. Except when the State Department finances a trip abroad, his company usually gives only sporadic and isolated performances, fre-

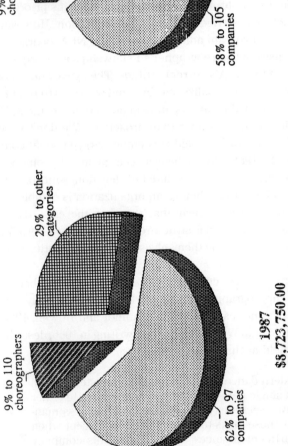

33% to other categories

9% to 97 choreographers

58% to 105 companies

1988
$8,852,000.00
Dance Program Funds

29% to other categories

9% to 110 choreographers

62% to 97 companies

1987
$8,723,750.00
Dance Program Funds

The Division of NEA Dance Program Funds

compiled by Keith R Bunganer

Source: National Endowment for the Arts
Annual Reports 1987, 1988

quently requiring travel for a single performance to some distant campus (the colleges being for him a prime source of audiences). He will typically operate a dance school or serve as a visiting faculty member at a college as a means of livelihood, and a desk, telephone and typewriter just outside his dance area may serve as his office. The studio— equipped at the choreographer's expense with a special floor— may be on the top story of a slum walk-up, because the rent is low and dancers have more endurance than cash. When an engagement is arranged, the choreographer must interrupt his teaching program and reassemble his troupe, whose members arrange leaves from the large variety of jobs at which they earn their living. (p. 31)

While there is still poverty among individual artists today in modern dance and many operations still center on the efforts of a single person, chances are that now, even the most solitary individuals have access to a nonprofit, tax-exempt corporation through which they can be eligible for funding. If the corporation is not their own, it belongs to a colleague or it is made generally available through membership in a dance service organization such as New York's Dance Theater Workshop or San Francisco's Dance Bay Area.

Spider Kedelsky, a former dance company director and choreographer who has received awards from the Endowment both as a choreographer and as a presenter, has acted as a consultant to the NEA since the 1970s, and served on the Choreographer's Fellowships Panel for three years. Interviewed in September 1988, Kedelsky discussed the issue of institutionalization in terms of the current "pressure [on choreographers] to form a company, to file for a 501(c)(3) [tax-exempt status], to set up a board ... because you have to operate as a business...." He went on to describe the Endowment's influence in restructuring the field:

When the Endowment was first established by Congressional mandate, it played a very active role in defining what the field was about. For instance, when I started Dance LA [his company] ... in '74, I structured the administration of the company immediately to get its non-profit [tax-exempt status], to do a [specified] number of performances, so that it could qualify immediately for Endowment and local funding. And state agencies, for the most part, and even city cultural arts programs, and large counties, often structured their structures which came into being ... at the same time because ... they would then receive Endowment block grants.

So you have this whole infrastructure from the Endowment on down that was being created by the mandate for the NEA. . . .

Dick Netzer also credits the Endowment with changing the organizational structure of the field:

> In a real sense, NEA and the foundations have achieved much of what they set out to do in the 1960s with respect to dance companies: . . . [now] there are *institutions* [emphasis in original], not just makeshifts centered on the choreographer, organizations that have some degree of stability, are sufficiently respected to attract heavy private giving. . . . (1986, p. 19)

But Netzer goes on to raise the possibility of an unintended result, asking whether forming institutions and then giving them heavy private and public subsidy, affording them long seasons and professional staffing, might not "make for a hostile environment for the new and small companies which have been a principal instrument of the development of dance in the United States" (1986, p. 19).

The Financial Stability of Dance Companies

The institutionalization of dance companies has been promoted with the idea of making them financially viable and administratively sound (Hardy, 1986, p.76). To that end, the Endowment began providing funds for professional management in 1973. Throughout the 1970s, those grants were in a separate category, especially earmarked for that purpose. But from 1980 on, when, one assumes, the field was considered sufficiently structured, funds for management were included under the general "Dance Company" heading which reads "To help dance companies realize projects that best serve their artistic and managerial needs. . . ." Additionally, in 1974, a "General Services to the Field" category was added, "To assist organizations or individuals who provide services to dance companies, dancers, and choreographers . . ., or who increase the visibility of dance in their communities or regions" (*Annual Report, 1987*). In 1987, there were fifty grants under that heading, representing about 6% of the Dance Program budget.

The growth of the arts service field has paralleled the explosion of growth in the nonprofit arts field, greatly aided by the availability of grant monies (Goody, p. 154). In some cases funding criteria for dance grants have included specific administrative considerations (for example, requiring dance companies to have reliable management before being eligible for the Dance Touring Program). Funding for the service sector itself has been plentiful both from the Endowment and foundations. Kenneth Goody (1984) takes note of the enormous growth of the nonprofit arts field as a result of government funding, and the emergence of "arts administration" as a recognized profession. He writes that over the past twenty years, private and corporate foundations have begun funding the nonartistic aspects of arts organizations, largely at the expense of artistic projects. Citing data from the Foundation Center, he goes on to say that

> ... between 1978 and 1981 total foundation giving to the arts increased by 68 percent. However, [within that 68%] giving to what is labeled "general culture", a broad category of which administrative/service support is a major componant, increased by 450 percent. Arts professionals appear successful in securing foundation grants. (p. 151)

The "general culture" figure comprises one-third of foundation funds to the arts.

Although Goody does not have figures for corporate giving, he suggests that there is strong corporate support of these purposes too (p. 154). As early as 1971, administrative personnel accounted for about 17% of the operating budgets for theater and dance companies (Lowry, 1978). While no later figures for dance companies were available, the 1981 statistical report of the Theatre Communications Group notes that for 1973–1979, administrative expenses in nonprofit theaters rose sharply while artistic salaries declined from 29% of operating budgets to 24% in 1981 (Baumol and Baumol, 1984, p. 179). As Lipman says, our cultural policy has come to rely "for both the formulation and implementation of its goals, on a formidable bureaucratic class" (1985, p. 23). Certainly, the Endowment depends on managerial personnel to implement its goals, both within its own organization and in the dance field. These are the people associated with fundraising, development, marketing, and indeed, with decisions on what the contemporary image of dance shall be, and what will be brought to public attention.

Moreover, this group has a major impact on who will survive, since an organization's artistic viability is now measured by its ability to raise money. Lipman describes the process as a closed circle: "Money can be raised because the institution is financially solid and the institution is financially solid because money can be raised" (1985, p. 23).

In 1976, the Paul Taylor Dance Company had a crisis which illustrates this point. Paul Taylor, who had previously earned acclaim as a choreographer and performer, founded his company in 1955, and it was, from the beginning, a successful and sought after group. When the National Endowment for the Arts began its Coordinated Dance Touring Program in 1968, this was one of the four original companies included, and it participated for the duration of that program's existence. In addition, the company has toured abroad extensively since the early 1960s, often under the sponsorship of the United States State Department. It has long been well known and considered one of America's very best (Netzer, 1978, p. 136). Financially, however, the organization was not on solid ground. In 1976, Paul Taylor announced the dissolution of his company because he could not afford to continue meeting expenses. Today, the company survives because the NEA and the National Corporate Fund for Dance united to mount a rescue effort. Judith A. Jedlicka, executive director of the Corporate Fund at the time, explains the strategy:

> We had to make sure that Paul restructured his entire board of directors and took on people who knew about management and could help him. . . . There is a need for business people on these boards, a need for fundraisers, and a need for guidance in financial matters. Modern dance companies have lived from day to day, and only recently have the big ones had boards giving them proper financial management. (Mazo, 1978, p. 92)

Jedlicka's reference to big companies lately having proper financial management brings to mind the earlier quote from Dick Netzer (1986, p. 19), where he voices concern about the growing gap between the larger, institutionalized and professionally staffed groups and newer, small, more flexible, and historically more innovative companies. With the field devoted to the support of established organizations, he asks, does this "make for a hostile environment for the new and small companies which have been the principal instrument of the development of dance?"

The Decentralization of the Field

The growth of modern dance as a field has paralleled the general expansion of the performing arts. During the 1970s, in accordance with its stated mission of broadening the availability and appreciation of excellence in the arts, dance funding at the Endowment was heavily concentrated on aiding sponsors across the country to produce performances by professional dance companies through the Dance Touring Program. Begun in 1967–68 with a budget of $25,000, this program allowed four companies to tour for a total of five weeks in two states. By 1977–78, the projected budget was calling for a total of 440 weeks in fifty states on a budget of $1.9 million (Mazo, p. 89).

The provision of funds was for more than touring, however. Companies operating under the Dance Touring Program provided a residency and a brief presence within a community, teaching and talking about dance as well as performing. In this kind of situation, company directors had the opportunity to acquaint themselves with the communities they visited and talk to their audiences about their work while under contract for a fee which allowed—in fact, required—that company dancers be paid union (AGMA) minimum wages. Suzanne Weil, then head of the NEA Dance Program, said in 1977, "The program has made all the difference in spreading dance and giving companies a chance to work. Back in 1968–69, everybody was doing one-night stands" (Mazo, p. 89).

Until 1972, the touring program was restricted to companies which met the Endowment's qualitative (aesthetic) requirements. After 1972, qualification hinged on whether or not a company met a predetermined fiscal standard, judged by such budgetary information as salary scales and weeks of work, essentially measuring a company's professionalism through quantitative means. Under both sets of qualifications, the touring program operated on a first-come, first-served basis. Eligible companies would arrange their own bookings and then apply to the Endowment for a 30% subsidy of their fees, either for a one-half or a full week residency. When the DTP budget for the year had been spent, the program was closed. Each year, the NEA drew up a list of groups meeting its guidelines, and many sponsors then used this list in planning their annual concert series, since they could get a rebate on the fees of these preselected companies.

Spider Kedelsky noted a problem, even as he appreciated the results of the program:

> The problem with the Dance Touring Program . . . was having the list of approved companies and the imprimatur that it gave, and who was selected and who wasn't and you know—

that eventually blew up in the Endowment's face, but in fact, [it] was a good program because it got dance out of New York.

The question of aesthetic standards in this program was a volatile one, and in a sense, it speaks to that issue throughout arts funding. Advocates of standards complained that in the years without controls, certain communities had turned against dance completely because a company of low quality had been in residence. Critics argued that government has no business imposing its taste on the country and that the quantitative measurement adopted in the early 1970s was the correct procedure (Mazo, p. 89). The DTP did eventually return to standards of excellence, according to Jack R. Lemmon. During "the last three or four years of the program," a Dance Touring Program panel was instituted which developed a list of companies based on qualitative judgments. (When pressed for a more exact timetable, Lemmon said he did not know, that the DTP was "old history for us. Most of the files have been retired.")

The very existence of a list was divisive, serving to separate the field into approved and nonapproved groups, and effectively bearing on the touring possibilities for all American dance companies. Though division was bound to occur with any list, the use of quantitative guidelines had made it possible for companies to gain acceptance through budgetary and organizational restructuring. Under this system, it was within the realm of possibility for any group to meet NEA standards through its own efforts, though without doubt, the system which numerical standards imposed on the field played a significant role in establishing the perception of a relationship between economics and excellence. On the other hand, with the reinstitution of qualitative guidelines, the determination of excellence returned to the DTP panel, and control shifted from the companies back to the NEA.

In fiscal 1984, the Dance Touring Program, as such, was discontinued. Discussion about the rationale for this decision has not been publicly available. Today, funds for touring continue to be accessible to individual companies under the broad "Dance Company" category and to dance presenters themselves.

The idea behind the DTP had been that exposure leads to interest, and that an interested audience is basic to the survival of all dance companies. When the audience is small, a professional group of dancers cannot be kept on salary because there is not enough work, not enough demand. The field had to be decentralized so that the potential, nation-wide audience for dance could be tapped. To further this goal, in addition to the DTP, from 1972 to 1978 the Endowment had a funding category for "Resident Professional Dance Companies," defined as those groups with professional standards and goals residing in communities outside New York City. The NEA would, if a company met its standards, aid the local community in its support.

In 1978, Netzer described modern dance outside New York as an infant industry, and so, for him, the NEA effort to expose new audiences to the form was justified (1978, p. 136). DTP subsidy helped provide touring salaries for (mostly) New York companies, and public interest in the form developed wherever they went. As the audience outside New York grew, it became possible, with financial support, to be a dance professional in many cities across the country. As early as 1977, David R. White, executive director of New York's Dance Theater Workshop, a major support organization for dance, characterized the 1970s "as an era of prolific growth in modern dance, in terms of both companies and audiences." In that year, there were approximately 200 modern dance companies in the United States, nearly one-half located outside New York (Mazo, 1978, p. 78). Former NEA Chairman Livingston Biddle cites a later statistic. He says that, as of 1984, with Endowment help, the number of professional dance companies had grown "from no more than 35 to 250. Audiences have grown at similar ratios, with the audience for dance increasing almost 15 times" (Biddle, 1984, p. 94).

With this achieved, the Endowment allowed the demise of the DTP. Thereafter, the NEA lessened its emphasis on touring, encouraging companies to request funds for "projects that best serve their artistic and managerial needs both at home and on tour" (*Annual Report*, 1987). In essence, this allows companies subsidy for a home season and the building of a local audience, greatly enhancing private fundraising capabilities. Beyond that, as indicated by Lemmon's assertion earlier that the Endowment is at its best when it is reactive, the shift seems to be to a more responsive role, a retreat from actively shaping the world of dance. Though the agency does not explicitly note it, the initiative now seems to be with the field.

Impact of Funding Patterns: Influence on Other Funding Agencies

The NEA's Statement of Mission clearly sets out the idea that though the government has a role to play, private support for the arts is of primary importance. Livingston Biddle, chairman of the Arts Endowment from 1977–81, describes that idea as "A uniquely American approach ... based on the theme of partnership—between government and the private community" (1984, p. 92). He depicts the Endowment's role as that of a catalyst: by using federal funds to match donations from the private sector, the government is able to point individual and corporate contributions toward the arts in ratios of up to four:one.

Samuel Lipman, formerly a member of the National Council on the Arts, is not completely comfortable with this arrangement. In his view,

> ... official cultural policy has from the beginning concerned itself with maximizing official influence on how private arts dollars are to be spent.
> This policy goal has been accomplished by means of what is called at the Endowment "leadership" and "presence." In this context, leadership means the NEA imprimatur. ... The need for this official endorsement, of course, suggests a lack of confidence by the arts-advocacy establishment in the intelligence, artistic sophistication, and will of private and (most especially) corporate patrons. (1985, p. 22)

On the same subject, Joyce reports that former Chairman Francis S. M. Hodsoll told the *New York Times* on 10 April 1983 that "a principal role of the Arts Endowment is to confer a stamp of approval" that will have the effect of giving organizations receiving federal grants not only money but also a credential that gives them an advantage in the competition for private funds (1984, p. 31). Hodsoll is further quoted as saying, in a speech to the New York Chapter of the National Society of Fundraising Executives on January 20, 1983, that the Endowment is

> ... encouraging greater private support (including efforts of the President's Committee on the Arts and Humanities; greater leverage from our grants; and a variety of specific projects designed to recognize, inform, assist and advocate new private support for the arts). (Joyce, 1984, p. 31)

A few years earlier, *Newsweek* magazine had noted the catalytic aspect of the Endowment's role. On March 16, 1981, while reporting on the Reagan administration's proposed cuts in the arts budget, Jerry Adler wrote:

> The government's influence is far greater than its modest dollar contribution because it serves as an official impri-

matur of worthy endeavors. As the number of regional theaters, dance groups, symphonies, light operas, video collec-
tives, mime troupes and jazz workshops has exploded,
befuddled corporate benefactors increasingly turn to the arts
endowment to sort out competing claims. (1981, p. 31)

Artists themselves recognize the status-giving nature of NEA funding
and list their grants in resumes and biographies.

Joyce finds the implications of this process problematic:

The essence of our political system is political accountability
for the expenditure of government funds. . . . for the federal
Endowments to attempt to influence the flow of private funds
for the support of culture is to remove policy, spending, and
staff from public scrutiny. To do so is to short circuit the
proper process of open discussion and presentation of alternatives. (1984, p. 32)

He and Lipman are both wary of NEA influence, noting that groups
without government support are likely to have trouble finding private
funding. According to Lipman, "Today, in the case of a government turn
down, the very future of a cultural enterprise is called into question"
(1985, p. 24). Joyce writes that "those applicants who have been rejected
for government matching grants will likely be deprived of equal access
to private funding" (1984, p. 32). Joyce continues with this caveat against
the narrowing effect of NEA authority:

The more diversity, the more alternatives for the artist and
scholar, and the more likely we are not to have an ossified
culture. Private donors must be guided by their own tastes,
by their own judgments about the good and the beautiful,
not by reliance on the herding effect induced by government
jawboning for culture. (1984, p. 33)

The Nature of the Grant-making Process

In its *Five Year Planning Document 1990–94*, the Endowment makes
the following list of "major needs and opportunities" within the dance
field: (1) increased performance opportunities, (2) affordable space,
(3) improved salaries, (4) more time for both creative work and rehearsal, (5) better training, (6) more attention to preserving dance works,
(7) more and better managerial staffs, (8) audience development,
(9) increased use of live music, and, not least, (10) improved financial

stability and increased financial support. The Dance Program addresses numbers (1), (4), (6), (8), and (10) through funding; the others, it says, are areas for advocacy and special initiatives.

> The Dance Program will continue to make funds available in as flexible a manner as possible to accommodate the priorities of dance companies and choreographers. Initiatives to increase dance programs on television, to maintain and enhance touring networks, to increase performance opportunities, and to support the creation and dissemination of new work will be continued. (*Five-Year Planning Document 1990– 94*, p. 122)

The process by which the Dance Program makes funds available to the field involves the use of peer panels, long considered the most appropriate means of making qualitative decisions within the arts. Critic Camille Hardy, who has herself served on a number of NEA dance panels, describes this system as "emblematic of democratic procedures" (1986, p. 77). While the *Annual Reports* list panel members and grantees every year, nowhere in Endowment literature is there a description of how the grants process works, how panels are selected, what, if any, guidelines they are given, who decides the budget for the various grant categories, how categories are established, why some names appear on more than one panel and others not, etc. For Fiscal Year 1987, under dance, the *Annual Report* lists separate panels for Choreographer's Fellowships, Dance Company Grants, Dance/Film/Video, Grants to Dance Presenters, and Special Projects. In the appendix, two other panels are listed: Overview and Challenge. For Fiscal Year 1988, there was some reorganization and only five panels are listed: Dance/Film/Video, Overview, Choreographer's Fellowships, Dance Company Grants, and General Services to the Field.

Kedelsky, in commenting on the panel selection procedure, noted his impression that the dance program director "draws from a number of different sources and then has the responsibility of making a choice. And that's a very powerful tool." On October 20, 1988, the dance program administrator, Jack R. Lemmon, was interviewed on these questions. He said that the program director (Sali Ann Kriegsman, at this writing) selects a slate for each panel with staff and field consultation. Then, with qualifications listed beside each name, all nominations must go to the NEA chairman for review and approval. Limited somewhat by pragmatic considerations such as who is available when, the program director and staff work to compile slates which will satisfy a range of categories that, according to Lemmon, has "evolved over time," to ensure equity among the professional areas of ballet, modern dance, administration, arts patronage, criticism, and dance presentation. The list must then be balanced against geographical considerations and aesthetic points of view, also taking into account the need for an equitable mix of men and women and minority representation.

Sizes of panels vary and percentages from each category will differ, depending on the nature of the panel. For example, on the Choreographer's Fellowships panel, an attempt is made to include more artists; for Grants to Dance Presenters, more sponsors. Lemmon emphasized the importance of balance and asserted that the integrity of the Endowment rests on the fact that its panels are fair and unbiased and that they are perceived as such.

Generally, panelists serve a maximum of three years and approximately one-third of each panel rotates off every year. Some panelists serve on more than one panel at a time for the sake of continuity and broad overview, the same reason that most serve for more than one year. When asked about criteria for selecting panel members, Lemmon replied that the director and staff try to include individuals who are "the experts in their area(s) of expertise." In terms of dance artists, he said, it was inappropriate for the agency to include an artist who had submitted consistently unsuccessful proposals, though it would not be fair to tie panel selection to past funding decisions. Artists "whose work isn't strong" by NEA standards have no place on its panels evaluating other artists. The measure of qualification is excellence, as seen through the eyes of program director, staff and past panels.

Aside from the work they themselves have seen, panelists are informed by reports from consultants, who are also selected by the program director with input from the staff and field. These people are the eyes and ears of the NEA, attending concerts around the country and reporting back on what they see. It is important that they have good writing skills, Lemmon said, since that is how they make their reports. In the more than 1,200 site visits made each year, the staff tries to match the consultant with the work to be seen as well as possible, in order to match biases and avoid discounting.

Once panels are seated, the directions they are given are the Review Criteria printed in the *Dance Application Guidelines* under their particular grant category. For example, in Fiscal 1989, under Choreographer's Fellowships, only one criterion is listed: "Fellowship awards are based primarily on the artistic quality of a choreographer's work" (p. 8).

Kedelsky spoke about the panel's decision-making process:

> I don't think there are any absolute criteria . . . the judgments of what is excellent are . . . what those people sitting around the table bring. That's why the . . . Program Director plays such an important role, because he or she decides who those people are going to be. . . . I think excellence is defined by the people who sit at that table every time.

Kedelsky praised Kriegsman's tenure as egalitarian and having a broad rubric, but, he continued:

> In the past I've felt that . . . the Endowment has too often been heavily biased in both its grantsmanship and the thrust of its . . . programming. . . . The way that it structures its program in a sense becomes policy decisions. And who it puts on panels and who it's funded has had a very strong bias towards contemporary dance and especially a kind of postmodernist sensibility . . .

to the detriment of ethnic, tap, jazz, ballet, and other forms. On the whole, however, Kedelsky is supportive of the peer panel process:

> It's an imperfect system at best, but I think it's the best possible system. And it's not immutable. It will change, according to who's there and who's gone. I think there's always an attempt to balance out artists, administrators, critics, observers, teachers, so you get as balanced a point of view as possible.

Opinion among artists on the issue of panels is not always positive. For instance, in 1985, choreographer Alwin Nikolais spoke about the NEA to a conference on dance administration, recalling that "it was started . . . to aid the economic status of the artist." He went on to say that

> All of this started beautifully, and then it began to go downhill. Things went from bad to worse. The panel process was initiated. A panel of peers? What peers have the time to be on panels? Very, very few. So, who gets on the panels? The managers, the people who have special interests. You have on the panel, for example, maybe two for Modern Dance and two for Ballet, and two for Ethnic, or maybe three for the

Ethnic and then you must go into the various territories and make sure that the Midwest is represented, and the East and the West, and so forth. Can you imagine what a garbled bunch of opinions you can get out of such a thing, where the two Modern Dance types may be very much against the Graham ideas, or the Cunningham, or Nikolais, or whatever—and just those two can shout down the whole process of voting funds for a particular company. It is a most inequitable kind of process. (p. 5)

Dick Netzer agrees that peer panels are not necessarily a guarantee of fairness. He, too, notes the possibilities for conflict of interest embedded within that process, saying that agency

officials have a lot of influence on panel decisions because they determine the agenda and ways in which matters are presented to panels for decision. Moreover, the peer-review process itself contains inherent conflicts of interest. Almost inevitably, panels tend to look with favor upon activities that make sense to the panel members because they do such things themselves. Consciously or not, some panels amount to "old-boy" networks that respond favorably to applicants who are part of that network. As the competition for grants increases—and I believe it will—it will tempt advisory panelists to judge in ways that effectively keep outsiders out. . . . Arts grants-making agencies need to pay more attention to this issue rather than turning away criticism with the refrain, "But we have panels and peer review." One step in the right direction would be the designation, on occasion, of outside panels to review the panels. (1978, p. 194)

When Lemmon was asked whether seated NEA panel members are eligible for grants under their category, he replied that they are excluded only if they are sitting on the Choreographer's Fellowships panel. In other categories, dance organizations are not disqualified by having a representative seated on any panel for which they are eligible. If, for example, an organization has applied for a Dance Company grant and the company director is sitting on that panel, he/she will simply be asked to leave the room for the discussion of that application, and will not be informed of the outcome until formal announcement of grants is made.

Lemmon noted that applicant-panelists are allowed in organizational categories because a proposal by an organization involves the efforts of many people. Panel participation is not viewed as a conflict of interest because the decision will not directly (or particularly) bear on the seated

The NEA and Its Impact on Modern Dance   *43*

member in the same way it would if he/she were applying as an individual choreographer.

Lemmon also mentioned that organizational eligibility does not depend solely on the work of one person as do Choreographer's Fellowships; with organizations, there are many contingencies. For instance, in fiscal 1989, eligibility for a Dance Company grant involved legal requirements such as tax exemption and compliance with the Civil Rights Act of 1964 and other laws banning discrimination on the basis of race, color, national origin, handicap, age or sex, in addition to a minimum compensation scale for professional personnel, laborers, and mechanics on Arts Endowment supported projects. Beyond this, companies must usually have:

- a professional artistic and management staff
- at least twenty weeks of rehearsals and/or performances during the current year and at least twenty weeks during the previous year
- been in continuous operation as a professional company for at least three years at the time of application
- demonstrated ability to raise private and/or other public funds. (*NEA Dance Application Guidelines*, p. 11)

Because of these criteria, the Endowment has concluded that there is no conflict of interest inherent in having members of applicant organizations seated on panels which decide on these applications. The 1987 *Annual Report*, the most recent year for which data are available, shows that of thirteen panel members for Dance Company grants, eight list a company affiliation. That year, all eight of those companies were given funds under that category. On the Grants to Dance Presenters panel, four out of eight panelists list an association with a producing organization and all were funded under that category. The General Services to the Field panel of seven includes four with an affiliation to a dance service organization. All four of these organizations were awarded funds under that category. Further research would doubtless reveal more such connections in any given year.

Political Implications of NEA Funding Policies

Samuel Lipman believes that government support of the arts is mutually beneficial: "Government legitimizes art, and art legitimizes government" (1985, p. 22). Michael Useem writes about this relationship in more detail. In the mid-1960s, he says, when the NEA was established, the government was facing an upsurge in political dissidence and a decline in legitimacy. Useem suggests that spreading urban disorder and organized protest movements created a need for ideological control which "may have been a major factor behind initial government intervention in the arts" (1976, p. 795). He quotes Douglas Dillon, a former secretary of the treasury and, at that time, chairman of the Business Committee for the Arts, as urging corporate support for the arts in 1969 because "artistic performances of one sort or another are essential in handling the crisis of our cities" (p. 795).

Useem also mentions the 1965 Rockefeller Brothers Fund report which, he says, "played an important role in mobilizing federal commitment to the arts" (p. 796) because it stressed art's usefulness in modern society: "The use of leisure can be both an individual and a community problem if it is not channeled into constructive and satisfying ranges of activity such as the arts afford" (p. 796). Useem notes that he has no evidence of federal funds being channeled toward those artists most likely to produce art for ideological control.

Steven C. Dubin does see a link between funding and government interests, however, citing a connection between categories of funding and the nature of art produced:

> The control dimensions of both real and anticipated budget cuts are important. ... Their role in helping to shape the nature of artistic production is exemplified by the cuts in the NEA budget which were proposed since the beginning of the Reagan Administration. Segments of the program supporting nontraditional arts programming were specifically targeted for the severest cuts, for example, activities of minority artists, service to audiences relatively unexposed to art, and work of a socially or politically critical nature. The Reagan Administration has supported a return to traditional standards of artistic excellence, which means that experimental and critical artistic work will probably continue to lose ideological and monetary favor. (1987, p. 216)

Useem also describes government patronage as a source of change, pointing out that often money is distributed according to government priorities rather than priorities within the arts. He characterizes the process as having two stages. In the first, the flow of personnel and resources into areas of government interest is not sanctioned by the field, and those who undertake work on government priorities see it merely as a means to another end, as access to money which can then be used to further their own purposes. At first, cooperation is obtained through material incentives rather than shared goals. Eventually, however, government criteria are absorbed into the field. Well-endowed activities, Useem says,

> even if initially of marginal status, attract participants and develop their own networks and subcultures. In time, associations, training programs, ritual gatherings, shows, workshops, and journals emerge to institutionalize these areas. If through nothing more than their financial strength, these fields soon acquire legitimacy, and their priorities are incorporated into the broader paradigm of the ... artistic community. In this second stage ... cooperation is obtained ... through shared objectives rather than purely instrumental incentives. Government priorities are latently embedded in the paradigm. ... In both stages, the most visible impact of government patronage is heightened productivity in government supported areas and reduced efforts in others. (1976, p. 800)

An example of this phenomenon might be the policy of making money available to dance artists for school performances. This is an activity which the government has long supported as a means of broadening cultural participation. In 1978, the Endowment issued a statement which described its policy as one of suggesting, funding, and advocating educational programs designed to "enlarge and develop discerning audiences to enjoy, learn from, and support the arts." Exposing children to the arts and to artists was a major thrust of this policy. Writing in 1986, Pankratz indicated that the largest single federally funded program for arts education was the Artists in Education (formerly known as the Artists in Schools) program (Pankratz, p. 16).

Normally, high culture artists are inclined to work at what they find involving and to engage in a creative process which serves their personal interests more than those of an audience (Gans, 1974, p. 21). School performances require a shift in priorities, a reorganization toward making one's work understandable and appealing, and they require rehearsal time and creative and physical energy from those involved. Today, this kind of performing provides a reliable source of income for many modern dance companies and single artists, and it has become an accepted, often sought after, opportunity for work.

The same can be said for touring, a grueling, difficult way of life which was vigorously encouraged by the NEA for many years in order to bring dance to new audiences. Government subsidy has, over time, made travel an established means of support for many modern dance companies, enabling them to provide regular work for their dancers and opening the door to national renown. Today, touring is considered a mark of success in the dance world, though it requires performing for audiences which are often relatively unsophisticated and naive about dance.

In effect, these government subsidized opportunities have shifted artists' attention from creativity and innovation to concern with maintaining repertory and a readiness to deal with a large, unfamiliar market. As Useem says, the availability of money tends to determine priorities of energy. With an expanded audience, choreographers have had to cope with short attention spans, untrained sensibilities, and a lack of experience with dance as an art. On the whole, they have responded by trying to be more accessible, incorporating both the familiar and the spectacular, at the expense of exploring the form. Innovative work is by definition new and sometimes strange, frequently an uncomfortable experience for the general public.

On March 20, 1988, a Meta-Marketing Panel was presented in downtown Manhattan by Movement Research, Incorporated. Seated on the panel, choreographers Bill T. Jones and Stephanie Skura spoke of the considerations they face in addressing the broad, general public (their comments quoted below are all from the panel presentation). In response to a question about whether the audience was taken into account in making work, Skura said that in her case, she did not think so, but that she does give thought to marketing herself in a way that will be understood.

> I have great faith that if I'm able to manifest my ideas—
> really execute them in very concrete terms, that will get
> across. . . . After the work is made, then I give some thought
> to the audience. . . . What I am paying a lot of attention to
> lately is doing whatever I can so that the people who come
> see the work have the greatest opportunity to really perceive
> it fully and understand it. . . . That has a lot to do with going
> on tour because that is where the money is made, is on tour.
> And performing in New York City is very different than per-
> forming on tour. In New York City, everyone is very sophis-
> ticated and everyone has seen all the postmodern work in
> New York, and people know the work is referring to itself
> and other people's work. Like the piece I did tonight, "Art

Business," that could never be done any place but New York City.

Before going on tour, she tries to arrange for interviews in local publications which will appear before the performances. Skura feels that audiences need to understand the values and foundations of the work and the ideas, so that the strange new vocabulary of movement is not intimidating. In her experience, audiences sometimes feel there is a code they do not understand, and so are afraid to trust their own responses. Dances with no plot are somehow threatening, and having something in print can be helpful.

> When you're doing work that is so-called experimental or postmodern or new, what you're doing is new ... and you really want to communicate with people. ... I think it's really about communication. It's about new ideas. It's about opening people up to new ideas in their own lives.

In his response, Jones referred to "Secret Pastures," a recent work, "a controversial piece," which premiered at the Opera House of the prestigious Brooklyn Academy of Music. Jones said that previously, he and his partner Arnie Zane had

> ... been doing ... I think, quite vigorous, kind of postmodern "exercises" for a long time, stripped down works ... barefoot, in small spaces. Finally we were given the opportunity to do something big as we wanted to do.

At the time, Jones was interested in the visual art world and the melange of people attracted to it. In his discussion of "Secret Pastures" he spoke of his collaborators, painter Keith Haring, designer Willi Smith, and composer Peter Gordon, and of using them to interest people from that world and "yes, to—wanting to have a success and fill the place." The dancing ideas, he said, would come from him and Zane as usual, and the collaborators would contribute music, scenic design, and costumes. Jones spoke of the process involved with "Secret Pastures" in political terms:

> I think it was really, in a lot of ways, misunderstood. People thought it was just—to use a term in the Black vernacular— to get over. That we'd lost our souls in doing this work. For us it was an extension of what we'd always done. I thought, at that time, the avant garde was a little too taken with its austerity. I thought the true chanciness would be in doing

something that was accessible. I'm also a socialist. I'm also a black person who's been working for the longest time in groups of white people. I wanted to see what I could do—what do black people go see? What do people of color go see? What do working class people go see? So how are we going to package it? How are we going to present it? So we thought we'd do a quasi-narrative, something that was colorful and yet inside it was even characters that people could relate to. I wanted to create a character who'd be real sympathetic. I wanted to know what it was like when people care at the end of a movie what happens to somebody, rather than a cool, abstract evening. So in that way, we were thinking about audience....

But, he insisted, thinking in terms of audience need not dilute the work: "Everything you offer you should be proud of. And inside of everything, there should be some rigorous idea. There should be something that's going to have some meat to it."

Jones's inclusion of both creativity and communication as important values in his work appears realistic in today's world. That combination, however, seems a fairly recent concern among artists who consider themselves modern dancers. Earlier generations seem to have expected audience resistance, and accepted it as part of their work.

For example, Don McDonagh describes Martha Graham as often being misunderstood in the early days. Even on tour, she gave her audiences "what absorbed her ... and it was their job, in effect, to provide the rest of the experience" (1973, p. 101). He mentions concert after concert where curious, even sympathetic audiences went away somewhat at a loss. Graham "made no concessions. ... In Santa Barbara, as elsewhere, Graham had assaulted the eyes with bodily configurations that it would take a generation to become accustomed to" (p. 115). Eventually, the dance-going public came to embrace her vision. According to McDonagh, however, this staunch insistence on doing things her own way contributed to her legend. "Though she was not a commercial success, she had a moral integrity that gave her stature" (p. 103).

Daryl Chin (1975) discusses Yvonne Rainer's work in the same terms, suggesting that in spite of her philosophic objection to the heroic stance of artists in Graham's generation, she herself became a culture hero largely on the basis of the integrity of her aesthetic values. Chin writes that Rainer declared an adversarial position in regard to the culture early on, and as a result, her audience remained marginal, consisting largely of students and other artists. In effect, her integrity isolated her from the possibility of cultural co-optation, denying her work wide recognition.

Given these precedents, the NEA's rubric of "broadening the availability and appreciation of . . . excellence" and the concept of excellence itself are both ripe for discussion. Much has been written about the issue. Baumol and Baumol, for instance, characterize the drive for new audiences as both a path to more money and an "insidious threat to standards and programming and performance" (1984, p. 193). Lipman acknowledges the same phenomenon, though he bases his remarks on the perception that government support of culture has become a political tool, used by public figures to demonstrate their goodwill and culture, and to gain positive publicity. Since this requires an art which is generally perceived as good and worth supporting, the result, Lipman says,

> . . . has been a pronounced tendency to turn art into entertainment, to advocate those kinds of art that are already attractive to a large and expanding audience or can be packaged so as to appeal to such an audience. (1985, p. 22)

Dick Netzer notes a connection between funding and innovation. He points out that NEA critics complain about government support inadvertently causing small, creative groups

> . . . to expand their operations and undertake financial commitments that introduce caution: when groups become preoccupied with institutional survival, the need to pay union wages, meet payrolls, and make interest payments on debt takes precedence over creativity. (1978, p. 172)

Netzer cites a 1975 issue of *Alternative Theatre*, which discusses alternative theater groups in terms of their separation from the commodity culture production pattern, a withdrawal which allows the luxury of long, rigorous rehearsals enabling them to shape performance material to the life of the home community. Having very low budgets, they must work in "spaces" rather than theaters, and so evolve imaginative and inexpensive environmental design; by settling for subsistence living, they can show their work on their own terms. "In short," as Netzer sums it up, "poverty is good for the arts and government support is bad simply because the large size attendant on government support transforms the artistic enterprise" (1978, p. 173). His response is to suggest that the implied connection between size and quality be dispatched and that grants be made available for groups that do not choose to grow. In addition, he says that

> ... grant-making agencies should make an effort to dispel any impression that groups that do not meet the eligibility standards for public support programs—or do not choose to apply—are somehow inferior, nonprofessional, and not deserving of even private support. (1978, p. 174)

Kenneth Goody, too, speaks of the tension inherent in making art available to a broad audience base while maintaining standards of excellence and creativity, an issue which he says has been a source of controversy since the federal government became involved in the arts. He notes the growing politicization of the arts as attempts are made to increase public access:

> As government programs are funded by tax revenues, factors are considered in grant making that are not necessarily considered by foundations and corporations. This had led in part to intense competition for government funds by numerous groups. (1984, p. 153)

To illustrate, Goody cites concerns such as regional distribution and economic and educational barriers as being active factors in awards, which enable groups with political and social agendas to be eligible for arts funding, especially on the state and local level. He observes that growing numbers of arts organizations are engaging in the political process as a means of finding support, building constituencies within their communities, and evolving social arguments for justifying their work.

The duality which Goody mentions is set out in the Endowment's mission statement, which declares two goals: fostering excellence and broadening the availability and appreciation of excellence. Taken together, these goals raise deep questions: On what basis can the two coexist? For whom is art made? What purpose can or should it serve in American society? How can it attract a reliable fiscal base? And not least, what is excellence? Who decides? The 1965 *Rockefeller Brothers Panel on the Performing Arts* highlighted these questions early in the arts policy-making process:

> Popularization in any realm often leads to a reduction of standards. In our efforts to broaden the audience base, we must not be led to accept imitation as a substitute for cre-

ation, mediocrity as a stand-in for excellence. Democratization carries with it a peril for the arts. (Goody, 1984, p. 153)

The Endowment itself speaks cogently about the problem:

Concern continues that financial stability is being achieved at the expense of quality or daring of the art produced, as evidenced by a 'safe' repertoire and reliance on stars and blockbuster exhibitions. A related issue is the role of the artistic director vis-a-vis the board of directors in the governance of arts organizations. As the influence of boards who represent the community grows, their governing role will also affect the nature and quality of the work produced. Another related concern is the impact of market research and of quid pro quo funding relationships on the artistic product. (*Five-Year Planning Document 1990–94*, p. 4)

In some ways, this issue can be characterized as a conflict between the interests of creator and consumer, a delicate balance in any circumstance. The popular arts are, on the whole, user-oriented, existing to satisfy audience values and wishes. High culture artists, at the other end of the spectrum, have often been fearful that their audience will be tempted by user-oriented art or that they will demand what might be called a democratic-cultural right to be considered in the creative process of high culture (Gans, p. 63). Those involved in high culture have traditionally adopted a posture protective of the creator-orientation, arguing that because creators make culture their work, they should be in a leadership position rather than bending to the will of their audiences. Now, in attempting an expansion of audience, these artists are facing a clash of values.

Hans Haacke, a New York visual artist, writes about the problems posed, for artists and administrators alike, by the use of tax money in support of the arts. Popular resistance to certain kinds of art brings up issues of control. Who decides what will be funded? Haacke raises questions which he considers fundamental to the interests of a democratic society:

Should the population have a direct say in what kind of culture it supports with its tax money? Is it sufficiently informed to make sound judgments in its own long-term interests? And could such interests be served, in fact, by an art that does not attract a large public? (1981, p. 59)

The same ideas, in different terms, were discussed in *Newsweek*:

On the one hand, there is the neo-philistine argument, as raised by Boston lawyer and novelist George V. Higgins, who gripes, "I don't like the idea of a steamfitter [paying taxes to] subsidize a book of poetry. Tickets for the [New England Football] Patriots are $20. Should they be subsidized?" Taking a contrary view, an influential Heritage Foundation report to Reagan charged that the arts and humanities endowments "have compromised their high purpose by funding programs that dilute intellectual and artistic quality in order to expand their popular appeal." (Adler, 1981, p. 31)

Over the years, many artists have felt that the NEA ought to belong to those in the arts, to help with making work possible and with facilitating long-term goals, difficult enough in an increasingly commercially-oriented society. Yet, as Kedelsky says,

This is public money and that's something that artists ... tend to forget. The Endowment both is the sacred province of artists and it's not. ... It's still public money, paid by American tax payers. The panel just can't do anything. We do have to have guidelines. It is a federal government agency. ... it has a very specific mandate which is to support and expand the vision of what the arts can be in America.

Kedelsky has observed the role of the NEA within the dance world since the early 1970s. He suggests that, over the years, the Endowment has become less flexible as it has become institutionalized, and that it has now moved into a reactive stance in relation to the field. In the early days, he says, the mission was one of building the field, encouraging more work, more companies, and bigger audiences. At that time, the dance program was a creative force.

So you have, from the mid-60s on ... this massive infusion of money. You have to have programs to [decide] how these monies are given out and how artistic criteria are made, so all this was being put into place. And that affects how the field views itself, how it presents itself; it affects how presenters who get a cut of the pie ... how they see dance, how they judge dance. ... So the Endowment played a role as innovator, as pace setter, as an arbiter of taste and decision-making, as a model for state arts agencies.

Now, he says, the "mission is to keep as many people of excellence going as possible." There is less latitude for creativity within programs, as precedents have been set, and the field has come to expect a certain level and kind of support. Netzer agrees. He cites the more or less permanent commitment of large portions of the budget for the support of institutions which are "'hooked' on public support and could go 'cold turkey' only with considerable pain," resulting in an evolution of the NEA's operating style from entrepreneurial to custodial.

Many questions surround the issue of public funding. Some are posed in terms of the tension between preservation and innovation. Others ask for whom the funding is intended: should the money go for work that general audiences like or for work that satisfies artists and expands the boundaries of art? Tension of this sort is necessary and inevitable in a dynamic society, leading to creative and innovative solutions. The rapid influx of money into dance since 1965 bears examination, however. As new generations of artists are born into what has become an art market, will taxpayer and artistic views begin to converge, reducing the tension? It is conceivable that young artists will not question the marketing ethic because they will have known no other way.

Steven C. Dubin says that this is already happening. He describes the long-term effect of public funding and, indeed, all kinds of funding, as a socialization process, and writes that the uncertainty of continued support acts as a constraint, making artists less likely to offend. A process of implicit censorship has been set in place, causing artists to think in terms of work that will fit in. The relative rareness of censorship in the arts is not proof of freedom, he says, but only that artists know what will be supported and what will not. This effect takes place today wherever artists work, whether under government sponsorship or in the "free" market. In Dubin's view, artists are not in a leadership position; the only open question is whose standards they will try to meet: those of funders or those of the commercial world (1987, p. 157–158).

Increasingly, economic achievement is included in the criteria for artistic success. We already see this in the demands dancers are making on the field, in their expectation of paying work in return for years of disciplined study. We also see it in the demands made on young dancers, as modern dance becomes more technically oriented and company repertories emphasize athletic virtuosity in order to sell tickets. Inevitably, economic values are finding their way into the artistic consciousness, affecting decisions about life and work and influencing the course of careers. It becomes difficult today to remember a time when this was not so, and to understand the difference that funding has made over time in the lives of practicing dance artists.

Four Dance Artists:
The Perspective
from the Field

ELIZABETH KEEN: OCTOBER 14, 1988

Elizabeth Keen has been a dancer for most of her life, though she did not commit herself to a dance career until she was in college. She grew up on Long Island and began once-a-week modern dance classes at about the age of nine. By the time she was fourteen, her dancing had increased to two or three days each week. For her, daily training did not begin until the age of nineteen, when she realized that dancing was what she most wanted to do. She had gone away to Radcliffe to major in history and literature, but by the time she was a sophomore, she knew that her impulse to dance was far stronger than she had thought. After that year, Keen transferred to Barnard College where she could

Elizabeth Keen—1970

Photo by Lois Greenfield

be in New York and continue her dance training. Looking back, she says,

> I remember it as being a rather unhappy time because I was constantly running back and forth between classes—dance classes and academic classes—and I don't think I really did either end of things fully. I was always running out of class, you know—a lecture—five minutes early to get to a ballet class at the end of the day when I was exhausted. I remember saying to myself, "Your body doesn't know you're tired. Just keep dancing."

Keen laughs at that idea. "It's just you, it's not your body. . . ."

She graduated from Barnard in 1959 and over the next few years began teaching. During this period, she performed with Helen Tamiris and Daniel Nagrin for two years and also spent a year touring with Paul Taylor's company. Taylor wrote about that time in his book *Private Domain,* calling Keen "enthusiastic" and going on to say

> Her specialty is devil-may-care flights and fearless flinging around. Bones like rubberized steel with extra joints. Though attractive, she's not quite as pretty as the other girls, yet she's the only one with breasts worth mentioning. Underneath her bravura there's a deep pensiveness; also a strong feeling for fantasy simmers there. I suspect that one day she'll tap it to use for making dances of her own. (1987, p. 106)

Keen left Taylor's company at the end of one year. Already, she had views of her own and saw herself as independent:

> In the early '60s, everything got started down at Judson, and I would go down there and show work on their concerts and be in other people's dances. But I don't think my views were really completely in sympathy with what they were doing because I never wanted to relinquish technique. [They were] following philosophical ideas at a very naturalistic . . . level and even at that time, I was doing a lot of teaching of lay people and I didn't find lay movement interesting.

Keen wanted to work with trained bodies, even though, she says, at that time, most dances done in the Graham and Limon techniques were

> . . . practically pure cliche. Nobody was breaking any fresh ground and Judson was quite a breath of fresh air because it was feeding stuff in, feeding in theories . . . well, partly

from Merce [Cunningham], but really much more immediately from the painters and sculptors [who were working in the group]. . . . There was an excitement there, an anything goes attitude—as long as . . . you didn't do a contraction. Actually, the most interesting person . . . at that time was Yvonne Rainer. . . .

Keen describes herself during this period as "ambitious in a very foggy way." She was concerned with making a living and being able to continue as a dancer, and says she focused her activities on

> . . . showing my work, . . . attracting some attention, keeping my head above water. I did a Masters degree at Sarah Lawrence, and that was because my father tapped me on the shoulder and said, "You get a Masters, you can make $10 an hour teaching rather than $2.50 an hour doing market research". . . . He was right. I mainly wanted to keep going in the dance world.

The dance world was much smaller in those days. "There [were] always . . . group shows at Dance Theater Workshop . . . a slot at Judson. . . . opportunities always came up." She continues:

> I don't think I had very clear goals. I just was dancing and going to class and making up these dances. . . . The field was much fuzzier than it is now, even though people were doing the same things, in that they tried to get their work done and have it shown. There wasn't any touring network for emerging choreographers. There weren't grants. I never applied for a grant until 1972.

Keen was among the most visible and well-considered of the young, non-Judson choreographers in the late 1960s. Writing in 1970, Don McDonagh described the work she was doing:

> What unifies the scattered look of her body of work is a passionate emotional intensity and genuine feeling for movement. There is a pulse and choreographic shape to her pieces that conveys a self-aware delight in the act of purposeful motion. Though she has dispensed with technique in some of her pieces, she does not turn her back on it. Technique and its disciplinary requirements infused with emotional fire have been the source of her finest pieces. (p. 270)

Keen's attitude at this point, she says, was one of paying dues and making a place for herself. She speaks in terms of striving to be "worthy

of calling myself a choreographer," and having "to earn the right. ..."
"I was very pure," she says about her ambitions. "I don't mean that I
didn't want to get things and I didn't go after them, but looking back,
I was exceedingly unclever." Essentially, she was not thinking in terms
of advancing herself. There was a network of people connected to the
Cunningham Studio and to the galleries (where much work was being
shown), and to Keen, they all seemed more savvy and less naive about
knowing who to talk to, who to chum up with. But, she says, her choreography set her apart from these groups.

> I was not drawn to replicate Merce Cunningham. It wasn't
> that I wasn't impressed with him or didn't study there, but
> I didn't want to jump on that bandwagon. If I had been more
> attuned with that, perhaps ... [I would have] seen how the
> networks were set up and fallen into that.

She seems to have regrets and yet, ultimately, is confronted with her
own staying power: "I look back, I think I was very naive," she says,
"and yet I've survived in this field and it can't be pure accident."

Keen produced a New York season annually from 1966 to 1980. In
1972, she began calling her group a company, because, she recalls, "I
got wise to the fact" of grants and what was required to win them. She
formed a tax-exempt, not-for-profit corporation in 1973 and acquired
professional management in 1976. Being organized as a company ena-
bled her to hold a group together from one year to the next, keeping a
repertory in rehearsal. But it also required her to expand into areas
other than choreographing and dancing.

> [It] made me plan more ... made me look further ahead ...
> start keeping books and fill out forms. ... Because it was
> incorporated and you have to do those things if you're a non-
> profit corporation. You have to have annual reports, and if
> you apply for grants, you have to give them a three-year plan.

These procedural changes signaled a shift in values which Keen found
difficult to integrate into her concept of life as a dancer. She looks back
at the ways in which her thinking evolved:

> ... when I say I was very naive, I remember saying ... re-
> alizing, in the early '70s, ..."You know, I used to think all
> you had to do was to be a good choreographer. Now I realize
> all you have to do is know how to raise the money". ... I
> really thought choreography was all I needed to do—even
> though I'm a very practical person in many ways.

Because the emerging role of business in the dance world was not immediately apparent to Keen, keeping the books and thinking in terms of management and marketing were not a priority, even though, she says,

> I can do it ... I mean, I don't like to, but it's not this sort of weird activity that I can't comprehend. ... Still, I didn't believe any of that was important. I didn't understand "institution," "ongoing," ... "five-year plans". ...

She points to Twyla Tharp as someone who did understand, the model of success, a woman of her generation and experience who seemed to have the right instincts and made some good decisions: "You ask me who is not naive, I would say that Twyla Tharp is the least naive of anybody. I mean, she's a wizard of self-promotion. She's an entrepreneur."

Keen wonders if perhaps her own insecurities may have held her back, inhibiting self-promotion and the recruitment and use of a board of directors. "Maybe I understood more than I think I did back then and I didn't develop it because I didn't feel it was worth developing." She describes herself as a loner who found it difficult to ask for help, to lean on others and build the contacts necessary for raising money. Her attitude toward her work was out of step with the 1970s push to institutionalize dance companies: "I never thought of dance as a business, and then, later I realized it was. It wasn't that I wasn't responsible about what I did, but I just didn't have that sense of it."

The Elizabeth Keen Dance Company, she says, "was considered a moderately successful modern dance company." As director, she made a point of sharing dancers with one or two other companies, figuring out her schedule so that between the companies, the dancers could accumulate twenty weeks of work in order to qualify for unemployment benefits.

> The mark of a good dance company was if you could have twenty weeks of work and put your dancers on unemployment. And I usually managed ten weeks ... sometimes twelve ... [of] work that would be paid at a level to qualify them for maximum unemployment benefits. ...

It goes without saying that the company worked more than ten weeks a year, but only ten or twelve were paid, and scheduling was arranged so that the paid weeks qualified the dancers for top benefits.

The Elizabeth Keen Dance Company received funding from the New York State Council on the Arts from 1972–1980. The company participated in the NEA's Dance Touring Program from 1973–1979 and in the Artists-in-the-Schools program for two seasons, 1978–79 and 1979–80. Keen herself received a number of choreographic fellowships from the NEA. She thinks of those years with her company as both fun and relentlessly difficult.

> It was the agony of making out those grants—absolute agony of filling out those forms ... and not getting enough money and seeing how far you could parlay that money. And then the fun of making up new pieces, finding music and getting costumes designed, and getting the stuff rehearsed and keeping things going with the dancers, and learning about lighting designers/stage managers and who to get and how to organize things.

The Dance Touring Program, which was in full force in the 1970s, was an important aid to the field, in Keen's view. It provided a structure, "a way to operate that was very clear."

> It made me feel that the government was really supporting the field as the field determined it to be. Because what was on the list was what was in the field. Then, of course, they started ... bumping people from the list.

In fact, the quantitative guidelines for eligibility, through which Keen had qualified, required minimum salary levels and a certain number of weeks of work along with an established record of professionalism. These stipulations were not always easy to meet, especially for non-New York companies without access to management networks and the national press, and so, without the profile necessary to attract the attention of funders. But Keen did not have these problems and did not question the list at all until "they started getting judgmental." In 1979, when the NEA returned to qualitative standards, her company was bumped from the list.

Usually, a choreographer begins her/his career working with friends and dancers who are interested in the experience of the work, because usually, at the beginning, nothing is organized and there is little money involved. With incorporation and management, a choreographer becomes able to pay and she/he develops a different, more managerial relationship with the dancers. Keen talks about the evolution of her company and how personnel changes made a difference in the working atmosphere:

> I'd had a fairly steady company for five years, having to replace a person here or there, but never the entire company, which happened in '78. For a variety of reasons ... I lost all five dancers at the same time. I auditioned ...

and hired new people, "the best dancers I found available," she said. But philosophically, they

> ... weren't tuned in to what I wanted to do the way my other company had been. It was a real struggle. If I'd been really smart about it, I'd have just thrown them all out and started again. But that's hard to do too, to ... reteach your whole repertory. ... It's so much work and just so discouraging.

Management responsibilities and the constant care of the company eventually wore her down, and in 1981 she disbanded the group. Since the company had not supported her financially, she had had to teach, and so was not able to devote full time to company work. She describes the situation as a "Catch 22": perhaps, if the company had paid her more, she could have given more of herself to it and so become more successful, but there was never enough money to do that.

> I was very discouraged financially and also, just spirit-wise, I was very down. I felt like I was grinding out work and that the only kind of work that I could get, if I could get it, was Artist-in-the-Schools. And I found that very depressing at that time.

Disbanding the company was a difficult and painful decision. After a long, thoughtful silence, Keen begins quietly:

> When I put my dance company on the shelf—I didn't realize how much my sense of identity was wrapped up in being the artistic director of this company—the Elizabeth Keen Dance Company. I just said, "Oh, I'll stop doing this now. I'll work on opera, theater—I'm getting so much work there that I'm having to turn things down—and I'll let someone else do the producing." And ... it was deeply shocking not to have my company any more ... [even though] I had felt so over-burdened with it and I didn't want the responsibility of keeping dancers employed. Yet I had taken on that burden with its rewards and punishments, and felt startlingly alone without it.

Already doing choreography in opera and theater, Keen assumed that she would continue doing that, while maintaining her ties with the modern dance world by choreographing for other people's companies. The two groups with which she did the most work—companies run by Daniel Lewis and Clive Thompson—have since folded, indicating to Keen that the troubles she had with her company have been widely felt across the field. Today, her work in opera and theater is going well, although she continues to teach at a number of different schools. She says that, from the beginning, she has never thought in terms of making a living with choreography or performing.

> One assumed one wouldn't make one's money doing that. And in fact, that's been my assumption all along. Whether as a dancer or as a choreographer, I have never made my entire living from either dancing or choreographing. I've always made the bulk of my living from teaching other people how to dance and choreograph and enter this underpaid field. When I had my company I didn't pay myself anything. I spent all the money [on the] company and paid the dancers as much as I could. The company broke even but the dancers, I think, for what we did, did well. I paid them as much as I could. ... In the past two years I've made ... maybe two-thirds of my income from choreographing and it's the best I've ever done, and I don't know whether this will continue.

Now, at fifty, she is concerned about her future. As a consequence of maintaining her independence and working as a freelancer at part-time and short-term jobs, she has accrued no pension rights. There is no easy answer to this problem. She talks in terms of going back to college for an advanced degree, or applying for full-time academic work "five years from now," and then reminds herself that one has to pay into a retirement fund for awhile in order to get something out of it. Clearly, her present career in freelance theater and opera work is both exciting and interesting to her; it is, in a real sense, the center of her life, even though she sometimes longs for total artistic control again. But she is not feeling secure. Next year, for instance, she says that she has fewer than usual jobs lined up.

> I think surviving as a dancer-choreographer from cradle to the grave is a joke, in terms of ... minimum security, so that you're not ... one of the homeless. ... Maybe the field stays so young—number one—because it's a physical field and— number two—because you can't continue in it if you want

to survive on any kind of even very low normal basis, to provide for yourself, unless you luck out and find financial security with marriage or have an entree to money some other way.

The issue of money in a field used to doing without brings up contradictory feelings. Many dancers, she thinks, are chosen by dance, addicted perhaps. Those who stay in the field often view their work as a calling. "People dance because they have to. They're compelled to do it. I was compelled. I didn't feel like I was my real self unless I was dancing." Viewed in this light, the financial problems which plague dancers and choreographers are not something about which they have any choice. They are, rather, accepted as the price for being oneself and fulfilling deeply felt needs.

Keen is philosophical about money. She thinks that the influx of funding in the 1970s was absolutely a good thing for dance. At the time, she says, access to money changed her perception of what she was doing. "It began to feel more like a real job—more like a profession rather than just a love, an amateur love. . . ." She implies that there is a developmental artistic progression which having money allows:

> Everybody can do pieces without costumes. Or, for that matter, without lights, and they can still be very good pieces. But, the more involved you get in the field, the more you want the right appearance of things, the right—not . . . window-dressing, but you want the work seen in the proper lighting. . . .

Money allows choreographers to present their dances in the best way possible, according to Keen, with a cohesive group of dancers and appropriate lighting and costumes. And it allows dancers dignity.

> It is enough for a person who is a dancer to go to class and to rehearse and to perform. That's a life. . . . That can be a very full life, to give that kind of energy to your dancing without having to wait on tables. Why shouldn't you be paid? I mean, the product, if you want to call it that, the performance that results is worth going to. . . . I mean, should novelists be paid to write a book? It seems to me it's the same question.

At the same time, however, she acknowledges that a salary may come to replace ideals in the professional world or get in the way of seeing the life as a calling. If dancers expect to make a living dancing, then they will "have to find a company that can support them," she says. And though "it may not be the way they really want to dance," for Keen, being able to find work within the field is the important thing. "Why shouldn't dancers earn money?" she asks again.

> Is it going to make them do less? ... Will choreographers choreograph less because they earn money doing it? Maybe it becomes less pure, or maybe—the only thing about money is, do you then start doing things because you think this is what will get you your grant? And I think there's some of that. I did things very balletically for awhile because I thought the way to get more money was to have a ballet company take this piece. I'm sure that influenced me. But then, for awhile, the whole field was going very balletic.

It is interesting to note that three months after the original interview, in a phone conversation, Keen raised this subject again. She had been thinking, she said, about whether "money spoils things . . . and I think in some cases it does, but it doesn't have to." Even in modern dance, she said, in recent years some dancers have become more like mercenaries, taking work with companies which can pay, without regard for the philosophical and aesthetic impulses behind the choreography. They have become gypsies, just like dancers in the commercial world. This can be a problem according to Keen, because in her view, the individualistic nature of modern dance requires that dancers be sympathetic to the artistic ideals of the choreographer. For Keen, this is a moral issue, an issue of commitment, which in no way calls into question the right of dancers to be paid for their work.

When asked to compare what she sees of the modern dance world today with the time when she was getting started, Keen says:

> The '80s definitely move faster than the '60s. We did have more time to develop. Now it's very much flavor of the year. ... People really need to work at developing themselves ... before they're recognized, and then perhaps don't need to be recognized quite so much so fast. ... I think we all have weathered these storms where you get noticed because you're new and then you just have to keep plodding on ... and people say, "Oh, shrug, shrug, we've seen that before." And then you keep developing and then all of a sudden they turn around and look again and see you're somewhere else and say, "Oh yes, she does that ... well."

Keen sees the major influences in today's choreography as contact improvisation, social dancing, gymnastic training, and ballet, all technical skills. In some ways, she says, "people are going for surface rather than depth," although emotion is returning, along with words; perhaps dance is drawing closer to theater. Ultimately, she seems to be saying, this is a difficult time for the art, a time of confusion, without clear direction.

> I think there's so much going on in the world today that maybe dance feels superfluous. There's such political trauma in the world . . . having lived in the world with the bomb and Viet Nam, these terrible, terrible wars in the Near East—and the Far East. . . . How does dance speak to this time? I don't know. . . . What does it pick up on in this culture? How does the culture manifest itself? Sometimes it's in the way people move. I mean, is minimalism and repetition—is that just a way of trying to make things stand still because the world is going so fast, changing so fast . . . ? [Is the response, in this case,] to build a structure against that? . . . One thing flowing into another—does this reflect the fact that we spend so much time watching television? . . . On the other hand, there's this great respect for the tradition of the ballet. Certain pas de deux are always the same. . . . Audiences are very happy to watch these things. They're comforting things, like lollipops—exalted, artistic, technically demanding, and therefore thrilling lollipops. Does dance—does art reflect the world or is it a safe place away from it? A representation of something that is not enough in evidence?

The depth of Keen's probing is notable, as is her clarity of thought and personal honesty, her devotion to making a life in dance, and the undertone of resignation. A career born of love and enthusiasm has matured with the evolving culture; dance has formed the core of her life for many years. Her early remarks about division within the self, her feeling of having been divided, first between academic classes and her dancing, between her body and soul, and then in having to split her energy between her company and earning a living seem to point up a constant in her life. Now, she teaches at three different schools and operates as a successful choreographer and movement consultant for theater and opera, frequently traveling across the country and to Europe to do her work—still divided.

How does one make room for the private in all this public activity? "I think I live alone because I'm a loner," she says, "not because I'm a choreographer or because of the nature of the dance field." Keen denies that dance has influenced her personal choices, but she does acknowledge that dedication and devotion to dance can preclude involvement in much else. Dancing can be a world in itself, she says. A dancer's life,

> ... it's almost like that of a religious fanatic, in a way. You devote yourself to being ready to do all these things. Because your body is your instrument ... the rest of your life [goes] on hold.

Kathryn Posin: October 16, 1988

Posin and Keen have been friends and colleagues throughout their careers. As people they are quite different: where Keen is calm and reflective, Posin is buoyant and anecdotal. She maintains a loft in New York City where she lives and rehearses, and at forty-five, Posin continues to perform with her company.

Like Keen, she entered the professional field before it organized itself around the concept of arts funding. She graduated from Bennington College in 1966 and came to New York, where, almost immediately, she began two years of performing with Anna Sokolow. Choreography was Posin's main interest, however, and right away, the response to her work was strong. Even in her earliest concerts, she says,

> I was getting very good reviews and good audiences, and the dancers loved doing it. And actually, the first time I ever saw [*New York Times* dance critic] Anna Kisselgoff's byline ... she reviewed me and said great stuff.

From the beginning, Posin received encouragement from all sides. Bennington had awarded her a choreographer's grant, and early on, she won a Doris Humphrey Fellowship from the American Dance Festival. These were years marked by major successes and strong connections. Then, she recounts, in 1970,

> Stuart Hodes, who was head of the New York State Council on the Arts, called me one day and said, "We have grants." I said, "Grants? Oh, you mean you give money." And he said, "Yeah, the New York State Council on the Arts gives money to dance, and we have a few left over $1,000 grants, but you can only get $999 because of a legal hitch. Do you want one?"

Before that, she had been choreographing on friends, and producing

Kathryn Posin—1979

fairly regularly. The offer of NYSCA funds came as an unexpected bonus. After accepting, she says, "I called up all the same dancers who'd been with me last year and they all wanted to do it again, but this time we could pay them. ... So there was $999 ... that was, like, incredible."

When the time came to submit an application for the following year, Posin recalls that she was uncertain about the procedure. "The boyfriend at the time" was David White, now executive director and producer of Dance Theater Workshop. In those days, White was also dancing in Posin's dances, and he volunteered to complete the application for her.

> David did my application. ... Then when I went in [to the NYSCA office] to review it ... my grant application was enlarged and taped on the wall at New York State Council on the Arts as *the* way to apply for a grant. And it was David. And David let slip that when he graduated from Wesleyan, they gave occupational placement tests, and that he had scored so high in business that Harvard and Yale had called him ... and wanted to give him scholarships. And he said, "No, I want to dance."

White handled all Posin's grant applications and company business for several years, until their relationship ended. "I think that's why I got off to such a very good start," she says.

> He danced with me, but he began to realize he was a better business person. ... He'd started too late. His mind was too alive and excited by all the other aspects to stay in the dancing.

After leaving Posin, White went on to take over the leadership of Dance Theater Workshop, turning it into a comprehensive, pioneering service organization for the modern dance field. He has continued to expand its operations throughout the 1980s.

Posin's career continued its upward swing during the 1970s:

> I became what I somewhat jokingly talk ... about—the flavor of the month. For years—about '72 to '79—my dance company got—one year it got both a [choreographic] fellowship and a company grant ... from the NEA, and it got lots of money from NYSCA, and it was on the Dance Touring Program. And we went all over the country. I kept the same dancers, so from about '72 to '79, we toured and we were a hot company.

There were seven in the group.

It was great, and I assumed that it would always be just like that . . . that I would make up dances in my loft, that I would get grants from NYSCA and NEA, that I would do a little guest teaching, but that I would have this great company that was a hot ticket, . . . and did interesting and innovative stuff. And that everything would just keep going.

In the late 1970s, Posin was awarded a prestigious Guggenheim Fellowship for choreography. At about this time, however, things began to change. As Posin tells it, she had a fight with her leading dancer which led to bitter feelings and a split within the company. To make matters worse, during this period, for the first time, a grant did not come through, probably, she says, from the NEA. Suddenly, her confidence was shaken.

I started to lose the loyalty of dancers who'd stayed with me seven years, and I started to have a lot more self-doubt. And I started to do, in my opinion even, not as strong choreography. And I started to look around and see other, younger companies getting attention.

The years around 1980 marked the end of the boom now commonly called the dance explosion. Ronald Reagan had been elected president and federal support for the arts was being seriously questioned. In addition, the Dance Touring Program was coming under intense scrutiny at the NEA. During the 1970s, the Kathryn Posin Dance Company had been a highly successful company: its top yearly budget had been $120,000 with twenty weeks of touring and eight weeks of rehearsal. With summer teaching jobs, Posin recalls, it was almost a year-round job for her and sometimes for her leading dancer.

The 1980s, however, brought a nationwide decline in demand. In addition, the company began suffering from internal disorders. After the initial group had begun to break up, Posin had hired an entirely new group except for two, and did not know the new people well. On one occasion, several of them were late for a flight and missed the first performances on a scheduled tour. The company reputation suffered, according to Posin, causing a further drop in bookings.

So then, very frankly, NYSCA stopped giving me money completely. And they still haven't ever given it to me since . . . about '80. And then the NEA kept giving me money but would every now and then not. So I started to self-produce, but there was . . . much less touring and everything started to look like not so much fun any more.

Even though company work was becoming discouraging, Posin's reputation continued to gain her opportunities for freelance choreography. Over the course of her career, she has set work on a long list of ballet and modern dance repertory companies, including the Alvin Ailey American Dance Theater, the Netherlands Dance Theater, Ballet West, the Eliot Feld Company, Juilliard student groups, and Utah's Repertory Dance Theater.

> So while the company . . . was touring way less, my freelance choreography thing was taking off. Then that started to get shaky too, because basically, with those companies that look for modern choreographers, you're good for one piece with their company and then they look around for the next newsworthy.

Posin continued to focus on maintaining her company, though she was experiencing increasing difficulties. She tells of a conversation in the early 1980s with Charles Reinhart, director of the American Dance Festival, which speaks to the problem of no longer fitting neatly into an easily recognizable category. Posin asked him why her company had not been booked at ADF recently.

> And he said, "You're in an interesting position. . . . I have funding for emerging choreographers, for postmodern, new stuff—Pooh Kays and Stephanie Skuras and Stephen Petronios—and . . . I get [make] money from the Paul Taylors, Pilobolus's, and Merces, but I don't have any place for your company." Which was a company that's already emerged and is having a little bit of a rough time and the work isn't clearly postmodern nor is it commercially viable, like Paul Taylor. He said, "You're in an interesting position and I'll be very interested to see what happens to you." And I said to him, "Thanks . . . this and one dollar will get me in the subway Charlie." So then I started to get depressed and lose even more confidence, although I kept working.

From 1984 to 1986, in order to support herself, Posin took a job at the University of Wisconsin-Milwaukee, but she did not give up her New York-based company. The university "poured about $40,000 into my company," she says, "and produced it there, and made it possible for us to produce here." She was not happy living in Milwaukee, but she stayed in order to support her New York loft and company, and only left Wisconsin when the department folded in 1986. From the beginning, she had questions about living a life which was so segmented. "It definitely reflected in the work." Even with annual performances in New York, bookings for the company dwindled to nothing, and, she says:

> It started to not look like it made much sense, except that I knew I wanted have a company because it was like my right hand. It was like the only way I could give an outlet to all the time I spent alone in the studio.

In the fall of 1986, Posin accepted a job at the University of California-Los Angeles while continuing to work with her company in New York, though because of the distance, the company work proceeded "with unbelievable difficulty." She stayed in California for two years before deciding that she had to live in or near New York in order to maintain a relationship with her dancers and sustain the contacts necessary to doing business in the dance world,

> . . . because I think the problems, even in the work itself, have to do with being too split up in your geography and in the location of where you work and where the dancers are, and where all your contacts are.

Press coverage at the time reflected the difficulties. On January 18, 1987, the *New York Times* ran a review by Jennifer Dunning which read:

> The Joyce Theater gave a performance Friday night, but the choreographer of honor seemed conspicuously absent. The program by the Kathryn Posin Dance Company . . . proceeded from one trivial or poorly thought-out dance to another, performed with an understandable lack of conviction. What has happened to the Kathryn Posin we came to know in the 1970s, whose work was full of energetic life if not of particularly well realized ideas? (p. A-50)

When interviewed in 1988, Posin had a one-year appointment at Trinity College in Hartford, Connecticut. She lived in New York three days each week. Though not permanent, this situation suggests the possibility of a manageable solution. "So now where I am," she says,

> . . . is a company with an operating budget of about $40,000, a location that's much more workable, and a feeling that something much better is happening, artistically, personally, but not economically. But I've come to the conclusion that the dance world, in terms of smaller size companies—not big ballet companies and modern companies—is based to a very faulty degree on newness and fashion. . . . And that there's

nothing I can really do about it except by doing good work and by still surviving, reverse the situation in my case. I can only do what I can do. But I find it to be a very bad flaw and I find that things like *DanceMagazine* and [its late editor] Bill Como do not help it. It's like, if you're not young and new and with a punk hair cut and doing something called postmodernism, you should die. And people who fit in that category with me are Phyllis Lamhut, Dan Wagoner, Gus Solomons, Bill Evans. . . .

Though she talks in terms of a flaw in the dance world, Posin also searches herself and her work, seeking factors which may have contributed to her decline, and she readily offers personal unhappiness and emotional instability as probable causes. "I was too split up and too upset to really be able to do good work," she explains. The combination of making a big splash at the beginning and then being superseded by young, new choreographers

... has contributed to my having a somewhat hard time economically and artistically. However, I take responsibility for the situation. ... And I think it's going to be very interesting to try to reverse it. Because, unlike Ze'eva Cohen and Liz Keen, I have no desire or intention to put my company on the shelf. I think it's neat. I like it. I believe in it. I've seen some wonderful things that I could do—I can just feel them right at my fingertips.

Currently [1989], she is working with seven dancers, paying them $300 per week for rehearsals and $475 for performances, though there are no grants so far this year. "I always pay them," she says. In the spring the company will self-produce a one week season at St. Mark's Church in Manhattan on a barebones $20,000 budget. In addition, they have one out-of-town booking in Kansas City. Posin will pay for this activity with the money she earned at UCLA, along with help from her board of directors, and, she adds,

I'm going to have to ask my parents for a very large amount of money. And they'll probably give it to me, but only if I promise to get a Masters [degree], because they're an academically oriented set of parents.

She considers her background part of her problem. Growing up with "a father who is a philosopher and astronomer and a mother who baked cherry pies, and nobody knew anything about money," did not prepare her to think in terms of business. Like Keen, Posin points to Twyla Tharp as "the single most successful person drawn from our mold," and notes that she has heard that Tharp's mother ran a string of drive-in theaters, so "Twyla knows from change. ... Twyla's like got the market on her mind from the moment she was walking. ..."

Of herself, Posin says, "I don't have a very good grip on economics," which she counts as a serious flaw. "In the field, if you don't have your financial act together, drop dead. Which is what I almost did." But she also links her problems to American culture in the 1980s:

> With the arts being so low a priority as they are in the age of Reaganomics, somebody in a not-for-profit art form, like me, cannot survive with such a naive attitude as worked in '72 when I was flavor of the month and there was a Dance Touring Program.

The general tenor of the dance world has changed over the course of her career, she thinks, resulting in increased economic pressure on dance artists today.

> The economy is more important in relation to the work, the quality of the work, than it used to be. And it means that I have to figure this thing out better than I have, and I haven't. And one reason I haven't is that I spend all my time commuting to Trinity College to earn a living to keep my company, to keep my loft. ...

When asked if she has any ideas about how to make things better, Posin points to the European model and says, "I think that there should be ... state-subsidized dance companies." She notes that there are Americans, William Forsythe and John Neumeier among others, being paid to do work in Europe. Here, in the United States, she says,

> An environment needs to be created where people can fail, like I have a few times, and do wonderful shit that's flawed, like I have a few times, and not fall apart. Where there's a little ongoing support.

Judgments about who gets support should be made, she thinks, on the basis of past work, including aspects such as integrity and survival.

In the current climate, Posin finds herself on the outside and feels that the modern dance field has been little or no help to her in her recent troubles. David White and DTW have not produced her work in five years, claiming that it is too balletic and too proscenium-oriented for their small theater. "It doesn't help when people like Charlie [Reinhart] and David—who do have some say so—are always looking for fashion and newness." With both, she thinks newness rather than past contributions counts, and she means newness to the scene rather than aesthetic newness. Both White and Reinhart have "unbelievable power," and, she thinks, "so does Harvey Lichtenstein" of the Brooklyn Academy of Music. Her old connection to David White is no help to her today.

> When I go out to lunch with David White and ask him to come to my concerts and see if he'd like to produce me, I feel like I'm his old immigrant aunt and he's ashamed of me and would shut me in the closet if some yuppies came down the street. . . . I'm tired of that feeling.

And the situation is not much different with other New York presenters. Going down the list of informal, affordable Manhattan performance spaces, including PS 122, the Kitchen, and St. Mark's, she says, "When I talk to them about producing me, they all say 'No, you're not what we're doing.'" Being "postmodern" and young, she notes, or having a historic connection with the Judson Dance Theater helps immeasurably in becoming visible and accepted in the New York modern dance world. Posin cannot claim any of those attributes. As a result, she is beginning to look elsewhere for opportunity and satisfaction.

> I wander into the ballet world more and more . . . in terms of the companies that I'd like to work with, in terms of my vocabulary, and in terms of my friends. Like I use ballet dancers in my company. I use a much more balletic vocabulary than I used to. I take ballet classes. And I'd rather go see the New York City Ballet than Martha Graham. . . . Because I like the [ballet] vocabulary better, and since I'll never be a ballet dancer, it's very useful to me because I can use it to my purposes artistically. It's because I'm basically so different from it, that I think it creates a great tension to have it there at my disposal. Also, I think I'm mad at the modern dance world. Yeah. . . . I didn't realize it till just now. I think I'm a little konked off at them. They're supposed to be my ancestors. . . . The ballet world thinks I'm cute and neat and has given me more money for doing choreography for them than any modern company. . . .

Posin is intrigued and interested by the world of ballet and commercial dance, but is, at the same time, realistic about the scarcity of work. As a result, she is trying to adjust to the idea of teaching in an academic situation, which is, for her, a more readily available, steady, and long-term source of income. Clearly, however, her interest lies in choreography and teaching is only a means to that end, "something," she says, "I'm doing just because I have the skills for it." University work has never really interested her. "The reason I keep having to shuttle from job to job, [is] frankly ... anybody who's ever hired me can tell that if I got enough bookings I'd be more than happy to kiss it off."

For all her struggles and financial problems, Posin does not seem bitter. "It's weird," she says, "but giving up is the last thing on my mind." She still loves dancing itself and works by herself, on average, two to three hours each day, alone in the studio. This may be part of her problem, she thinks, too much love for dance and choreography as processes: "My problem is that I just will spend the time in the studio and let the fundraising go." Blending dancing and creating with living still involves and challenges her, though she feels that the conservatism which is prevalent in this country today creates a difficult environment for making it work. Like Keen, she thinks that perhaps dancers will have to recreate a purpose for themselves as the culture evolves, so that dance will regain an urgency and a relevance to the times: " ... we're beginning to feel like we're not important—it's not just me ... and so we're trying to find some kind of value in what we're doing. ... " Her response, however, is a personal one, an attempt to integrate her life with the process of making dance:

> I have found, always in the past, that if the work is working and the people with you ... are working, and if you're in a somewhat stabilized frame of mind and can actually talk rationally to your manager on the phone, it does work. The years when it hasn't worked for me are because I personally have been unstable.

Ultimately, with Posin, it comes back to herself and the choices she has made. "It's really a question of balances," she says. "Trinity is a closer balance than UCLA. You know, it's like you just have to arrange stuff to work."

Today, at forty-five, Posin feels an optimism which has grown out of a long period of tribulation and self-examination. Recently, she says, she began to understand that there are no right answers, an insight which has brought both freedom and relief. Nobody holds the book. "Who am I trying to impress?" she asks.

Who is it who's smarter than me that's going to tell me I'm not good enough? Bill Como? [*New York Times* dance critic] Jack Anderson? David White? They don't hold the book. In fact, they all think someone else holds the book. And the sooner we all realize nobody holds the book or everybody holds the book, we'll all work better. . . . And that's why I'm not so upset about the fact that everything I've told you sounds like it's not working.

Posin says that as a dancer, her life, like many others, "has pathos. It has absurdity . . . it has stupidity. But it also has fun. I mean, I'm having a great time. . . . " She is not entirely positive about the future of the modern dance field though, or of individual dancers within it. Having been a professional all her life, she has few illusions about what is required for survival. Her advice to students says a great deal about her own experience:

I do always advise my students and younger dancers to not go into the field if they can help it . . . because I think it's a very bad idea to go into dance now, even worse than when we went into it, in terms of security, self-image, and sanity. . . . But I always know that the ones who need to do it . . . will do it anyway. So I try to get the ones who won't do it safely out. . . .

Jefferson James: November 27, 1988

Of the three women included in this chapter, James is the least like the others. Her life has largely been spent outside New York City, and for this reason, she has had to go about being a dancer in a very different way. Today, she directs, choreographs for, and dances in the Contemporary Dance Theater, a Cincinnati-based modern dance repertory company. She also manages its home, the Dance Hall, which houses a dance school, and produces a series of mostly modern dance events.

When she moved to Cincinnati, over twenty years ago, there was no modern dance community there into which she could slip. Her career has been involved with initiating and organizing activities and training dancers, ensuring modern dance a presence in Southwestern Ohio. She gives the impression of one who became a leader so that she could dance herself, and in creating a means by which to do that, she has also created a small repertory company, a school, and a performance space. She has functioned as a pioneer and a pacesetter, and though

Jefferson James—1986
in "Numerical Match"
by Shawn Womack

these are not roles she sought, over the years she has accepted the responsibilities with more and more enthusiasm. In a review for the *Cleveland Plain Dealer* (November 21, 1988), critic Wilma Salisbury notes the struggle necessary to building and maintaining a modern dance company in Cincinnati and remarks on the survival of the Contemporary Dance Theater

> ... for sixteen years under the tireless leadership of artistic director Jefferson James. In a low-key concert by the 6 member company Saturday night at Cleveland State University, James was front and center in two repertory pieces. Though no longer a young dancer, she projected qualities of strength and personality that gave the all-female ensemble its focus.

Salisbury describes James as "small and sturdy" and closes the review with the comment that the company "has a fine role model to emulate in the performance and personality of its devoted artistic director."

James began studying dance as a child and attended The Juilliard School in New York after high school. After two years, she left Juilliard and enrolled in the General Studies program at Columbia University for a year, taking dance classes at studios around Manhattan. Like Keen, she found this division of energy difficult:

> I'm not sure that I ever could have succeeded in getting a degree because it was too distracting to go to different studios all day and take classes ... and then trying to make the academics. It would have taken me ten years probably. I'm not sure I would have succeeded in following through with that.

She laughs. More than making her own work, she "wanted to be a dancer." During this time, she was enjoying working with a number of different choreographers, becoming acquainted with their processes and with the New York dance world. "I was going to dance," she says. "I didn't know with whom or what. ... I didn't have any great sense of having a leader. ... [I] wanted to find a way to do my thing."

Meanwhile, she had met a young music student, Martin James, at Juilliard. By the end of her year at Columbia, he had completed his MS and was hired by the Cincinnati Symphony Orchestra. Jeff James had originally planned to spend her life in New York City. She had, in fact, even rejected the idea of attending Bennington or Sarah Lawrence College because they were too far removed from the center of things. At this point, however, she married Marty and went with him to Cincinnati.

It was 1964. "I had no idea what I was getting into," she says now. There was very little in the way of dance activity in that city.

She began by teaching children. "Desperate to do something in dance," she gave her classes much of the energy she might have given to rehearsing and dancing herself. After a year, she enrolled in the University of Cincinnati as a dance major. Her credits from Juilliard were accepted and she would have received her degree within two years if Marty had not been drafted into the Army Band. This time they moved to Washington, DC, where, for two years, she worked at a desk job and did not dance at all. In the fall of 1968—her third year in Washington—she began a stint with the Georgetown Workshop, choreographing two dances and performing with the company for one year. At the end of that time, Marty's Army service was finished and they returned to Cincinnati.

In 1970, when James finally earned her BFA from UC, a small group of dancers gathered round her, all interested in remaining in Cincinnati, and willing to give time and energy to a fledgling company. This was the beginning of what would be CDT. The first challenge was to locate a space where rehearsals could take place.

> As soon as we found a studio . . . then we had to start teaching classes so that we could pay the rent, and it started to mushroom. . . . Holly [McCarty] and I were partners at the time. I don't think either one of us realized what we'd just gotten into. We were choreographing and we were making dates for these shows and we were trying to incorporate because we knew that we had to do that. . . . That took two years. . . . Holly dropped by the wayside, got pregnant . . . and after that, I guess it was all my thing. So I figured out how to get the corporation, went to a lawyer and got it incorporated. . . . In 1972 [we became] Contemporary Dance Theater and there we were.

James began applying for grants to the Ohio Arts Council in 1974 and got her first "tidbit" in 1975.

> By then we were committed to an ambitious four [different] concerts a year—a repertory series—and I was choreographing at least one, probably two new works for each concert, and sort of scrambling for new works from every place— from company members, from local choreographers . . . wherever I could find new works—and also having guest artists whenever we could.

She had established her group as a repertory company, which meant that the selection of dances would come from many different choreographers. In this way, she was not tied to producing work of her own, but could choreograph when she wanted to, while continuing to grow as a performer in addition to doing most of the administrative and managerial tasks the company required.

She says she did not have a plan, and that whatever fell easily into place seemed the right thing to do. She had not named the company after herself and felt no desire to stamp it with her own choreographic identity. Her training and background had been eclectic, and she says she assumed the company would take that direction too. Since she wanted the opportunity to dance and work with other choreographers, she brought in guests who would teach their dances and often perform with the company. "I wanted to dance, so I wanted ... many guests to come as choreographers ... and they always seemed interested." She reflects on how this has evolved over the years and notes that over time, the emphasis and the very language within the dance field has shifted to reflect the present focus on economics within the field:

> At the time I didn't think about providing work for other people ... I knew I needed their support in what I was doing and I figured everyone just enjoyed—if you enjoy dancing, it wasn't so much needing work. That's still true, that we all enjoy what we're doing, but it's also true that I'm very aware now when I'm giving somebody an opportunity to either have their work shown or to get their work to another place or to give them a chance to perform, that I'm making work for them. ... I know that [now] I think about it differently and that's one of those things that's so subtle a change—I don't know ... the way we speak about things has changed so maybe that's an indication that our way of thinking has. We didn't talk about it as work, we talked about them as "works" but we didn't talk about it as "making work."

The 1970s, she recalls, felt very different from today. There was a general feeling of possibility, and dance was involved and important in the community. Early on, CDT found a big space which allowed James to think in terms of presenting not only her own company, but other groups as well. Since then, the company has made several other moves, always to spaces where James could continue presenting. Over time, however, her sense of possibility and her place within the community have changed. In the 1970s, she says,

> ... everybody was thinking that there was no end to what we could do. ... We were just starting out. We had just made

a company and ... we had a space where we could present a little bit. ... There was ... an unlimited audience. We could seat one hundred people. We didn't have any trouble getting them to climb three flights of stairs and sit on hard chairs and come to performances. Of course, they didn't pay very much. They also had to park along the way.

None of these things would we consider having them do now. ... I'm afraid they wouldn't do it ... or the numbers would be so much fewer. [We might] still have one hundred people that would park blocks away and walk up flights of stairs, but [today] we need more than that hundred. And we've gotten more professional now. We pay dancers.

The sense of professionalism is new to the 1980s and as it has grown, it has changed both expectations and budgets throughout the modern dance field. In the 1970s, CDT was proud to be able to pay dancers anything at all, and managed by splitting the box office receipts according to the number of services performed: dancing in one dance, dancing in two dances, making costumes and dancing, etc. "It was very democratic" in those days, says James. Now, she says, when it comes time to pay, "you just sort of apologize because you know it's too little. ... A choreographer gets a choreographic fee. ... The dancers get an equal share: $100 a concert." If the company gets a particularly large fee, the dancers get more. There are no rehearsal salaries unless rehearsal money is specifically available from a grant.

James characterizes the 1970s in general as a proud time, and says that the biggest change for her has been the realization that she and CDT were not sufficient to the task of building dance in Cincinnati. She could not sustain the pace and the demands which mounting four different seasons each year put upon her. Moreover, she found herself feeling disconnected from the rest of the dance world and starved for seeing more dance. Given these feelings, expanding the emphasis of her work to include more presenting was a natural development. CDT has now become not only a regionally known repertory dance company, but a nationally respected producer of postmodern dance. By bringing guest artists in for several visits, alternately hiring them to teach, commissioning work for her company, and presenting their own companies in performance, James has devised a scheme which serves to acquaint Cincinnati audiences with out-of-town artists and to build long-term connections and communication between Cincinnati dancers and dance students and the visitors. "That's been the most exciting work for me," she says, the generation of new work and building connections.

Now she fears that the audience may be drying up. It is not yet evident from her own numbers which are too small to accurately reflect the beginning of a trend, but the larger Cincinnati performing institutions are noting a decline in attendance, and James worries that the audience may be stretched very thin at this point.

James continues to do almost all the administrative work for CDT and she has nearly stopped choreographing. Recently, her space, the Dance Hall, became one of thirteen founding members of the National Performance Network, a program begun in 1984. David White, of New York's Dance Theater Workshop, is the organizing force for NPN; he is currently listed as national project director. The idea was to build a network of groups around the country, like CDT, who already had a history of presenting. James describes the program as designed to provide financial assistance for the presentation of alternative forms of the performing arts—postmodern dance, mime, new theater, new music— work that does not already have established presenting patterns. In essence, NPN underwrites a one or two week residency by paying 35% of the company's fee. In hopes of encouraging presenters to choose the companies they want to present without the pressure of financial considerations, fees are determined by a formula applied equally to all participating groups. The formula for one week is as follows:

> $425 per person who comes (dancers, technicians, etc.)
> + fringe (insurance, social security, etc.)
> + $50 per person per day for housing
> + $30 per person per day for food and travel
> + airfare.

In addition, the company receives a $1,300 fee, whether the stay is for one week or two.

An NPN residency can cost the company which normally pays more than it would receive under these rates, but it considerably increases the ability of small companies to pay their personnel. The major benefit to large, established groups is exposure to new audiences and venues. Presenters have mixed advantages with NPN as well. For many, the required fee is more than they would ordinarily pay, but on the other hand, it brings some otherwise unaffordable companies within reach.

There is no list from which presenters must choose; any U.S. company is eligible for the program, though there are some restrictions. Normally, a participating presenter produces from three to five groups yearly through the NPN. Since one-half of the support money originally came from the NEA Dance Program, there is a stipulation that at least two groups each season must have won a Choreographic Fellowship over the past three years. The idea, James says, is to give artists which the NEA has honored greater exposure, an idea which effectively enhances the NEA's role in bestowing "seals of approval." White and DTW have further stipulated that only two companies each year can come from New York, which, according to James, sometimes stretches presenters, pushing them to search the country for interesting groups. Essentially, this network revives the Dance Touring Program, says James, but it has a slightly different emphasis, tending to serve newer, less established artists.

For CDT, membership in NPN has inflated both expenses and income because of the increased number of performances which it now presents. The affiliation has also given James' work as a presenter a legitimacy which would otherwise have been harder won. It "gave us a tie nationally," she says, "so that we can talk about what we're doing in connection with a national organization." Much of NPN's own financial sponsorship spreads to its members, so CDT as a presenting agent now has the tacit endorsement of large funding institutions like the NEA and the Ford Foundation. "We've used all that," James explains.

> It hasn't all of a sudden turned around the funding world . . . [but] they are gradually beginning to see that we are more important than just a little place in Cincinnati. We're important to Cincinnati because of our ties to elsewhere.

Additionally, James says, she and CDT have become more visible in the dance world because of the prestige associated with NPN. There is now a steady flow of unsolicited videotapes and press kits to the CDT office, sent from dance artists hoping to catch James' eye and secure a booking. She is perceived as having power, and indeed she does, as she herself acknowledges when she talks in terms of "making work" for performing artists. Moreover, "Because of this connection . . ." she says, "I have been invited to be on a number of panels" in various areas of the country, an activity she finds interesting and educational in terms of seeing dance on a national scale. These are the funding panels of state arts agencies, where James views videotapes of artists from that region and helps make decisions on grants. James is impressed by the wide variety she sees and is pleased to be part of the funding process.

Though she is still actively performing, James has gradually embraced a broad view of herself and has expanded into roles where she is in a position to have influence. Her circumstances and her locale have made it both possible and necessary. Had she stayed in New York, she would have had a career as a performer, and might not have felt the need to form a company since she has never experienced an urgency to choreograph. Becoming a presenter would have been both less necessary and much more difficult, at the very least because of the scarcity of suitable and affordable spaces in Manhattan. But perhaps the biggest difference Cincinnati has made in James' life can best be described in terms of scale: the sense of her own impact, which she experiences daily, is a satisfaction which New York rarely offers because of its size and scope.

Recently, on trips to New York, when she has talked with dance artists there, she has found, she says, that

> [among] choreographers, people who teach, people who perform ... the general feeling was of isolation, of working very hard and getting nowhere. ... I have, more and more, heard ... "I'd like to get out, get away from New York" ... and yet, there's a real fear of doing it.

Living and working in Cincinnati has allowed James to achieve, in her own way, career satisfaction. Life in New York, traditionally seen as required for a professional dance career, has become more difficult and expensive over the years. But still, artists stay because often, going elsewhere is seen as a break with a way of life necessary to art. Though a move might mean more space, more light, less fear, and more opportunity, for many, the idea of leaving the city permanently is like stepping into an artistic vacuum.

Through her own efforts, however, James has created a life in Cincinnati which compensates for the lack of a concentrated arts community. Today, at forty-five, she has found what seems to be an agreeable mix of dance and life. This mix, according to James, is one of the biggest concerns she hears voiced by artists living in New York—in her words, the problems of "how to live and do their work. How to live a reasonable existence and do the work they want to do."

Spider Kedelsky: September 23, 1988

Aside from being male, Spider Kedelsky is different from Keen, Posin, and James in a number of ways. He grew up in Brooklyn, the son of

Spider Kedelsky—1988

Photo by Robert Cavin/UNCG Publications

parents who had emigrated from Poland and Ukraine, an "unworldly" family, he says, where no one had gone to college. Kedelsky himself went to Brooklyn College where he received a BA in political science in 1966. Later, in 1974, he earned an MA in dance from the University of California at Los Angeles.

He began dancing as a young adult in the 1960s. For him, dance was part of a process of opening up to the world which led him far beyond Brooklyn. It quickly possessed him: "Dance offered great opportunities for social relations," he says. And more: "In terms of my own physicality, it just touched off a chord and I was gone. It was like a disease."

He started at twenty-three, for a year, rising early in the morning to make time to dance by himself—"freestyling it," as he says. At the end of that year, he attended his first formal classes—exactly three at the Joffrey Ballet School, which, he describes as "like a Martian experience." These were followed by several months of work with the New Dance Group. Eventually, as he grew more accustomed to the New York dance world, he explored many different kinds of classes, including those at other ballet schools and modern classes with Merce Cunningham and Alvin Ailey. Although he started late, he quickly and easily became heavily involved in the field. At the time, he was earning his living teaching grade school.

> Dance was both my individual passion and response to what I wanted to say as an individual human being. . . . I was always "creative and expressive" as a dancer, and I worked fairly soon, I guess because I was a guy, but also, I was a very good performer. I was very present on stage. So I was performing right away.

"But," he continues, "I always had other interests . . . in visual arts . . . in politics, international politics, particularly in . . . the non-Western world. . . ."

In 1971 he left New York for California, and enrolled at UCLA for graduate work in dance. During his time there, he became involved in founding Dance/LA, a modern dance repertory company. From the beginning, Kedelsky understood the national and state funding systems and knew how to operate to advantage within them. It was 1974, and Dance/LA was organized with NEA guidelines in mind, a direct response, he says, to

> the pressure . . . to file for a 501(c)(3) [tax-exempt status], to set up a board . . . because you have to operate as a busi-

ness. ... and I did fantastically well with Dance/LA. At its peak, in '77 or '78, ... it toured more than anybody in California. ... The intent fully was to set up a business which could function right away.

Though at the time there were other groups in California which Kedelsky thinks were more artistically talented, "we got the grants," he says, "because we were organized and that's the way it goes in America." After five or six years, the passionate involvement with dance began to fade. As he tells it, his discovery of non-Western dance forms—which he could connect with his interest in politics—rekindled the spark for awhile, and his relationship with mentor Jack Cole at UCLA held him to the dance world. But gradually, other interests began to interfere with what he was doing. In 1978 he left Dance/LA, he says, for a number of reasons:

> I had several serious questions. One was ... about continuing to be in Los Angeles, though I did stay there for, oh, five years ... more. I had a very serious question about whether I wanted to continue being in dance, which is a question that I still have. ... And there were personality conflicts. Dance/LA was a group of people who worked in the Graduate Dance Center at UCLA, who all had Rockefeller Foundation scholarships and auditioned to get into this special program. It grew out of that group of people. ... therefore, it had no common, philosophical artistic roots to begin with. ... And even much more than I am now, I was a very headstrong, very impetuous, very arrogant guy. It was very hard for me to get along in what was supposedly a ... collective when I was clearly the dominant figure. ...
> I was the first one to go. ... but I think Dance/LA still exists in LA.

Kedelsky became a freelance choreographer and presenter/producer, and for a number of years, he traveled "to mostly Third World countries, to see what the world looked like." As he traveled, he saw as much dance as possible, and set several of his works on a number of dance companies, including the Kibbutz Dance Company in Israel and the Aboriginal-Islander Dance Theatre in Australia. During this period, he was instrumental in bringing Aboriginal performers to the United States and touring the country with them as they presented their dances.

In 1982, Kedelsky joined the faculty of Amherst College in Massachusetts and became a member of the executive committee of the Five College Dance Department. He stayed for four years. Since then, there has been a year as an arts consultant, and a year on the dance faculty at the University of North Carolina at Greensboro. He was invited to return for a third year as a dance panelist at the Endowment, and was approached by the North Carolina Arts Council to serve on a choreography panel and to take part in a roundtable discussion on the future of dance in North Carolina.

When asked about his reasons for drifting away from the dance world, Kedelsky is careful to explain that it is not because he no longer likes dance: "I love dance. I mean, there's nothing that makes me feel more whole and complete. . . ." He has had injuries which make it difficult to dance fully with pleasure. "I've just gotten older, too," he says. But there are other reasons, having more to do with how Kedelsky, with his expansive range of interests, fits into the narrowly focused world of modern dance:

> . . . as I went along, I found out the people I was working with really didn't have much to say that interested me. As I grew more and more to know the form—not necessarily to master the form myself, but to begin to understand what mastery of the form meant, I realized how few either master the form or really were speaking to me any longer. And . . . as my sophistication grew, my interest in things that surrounded the field . . . began to take precedence.

"Why did I stop choreographing?" He pauses. He thinks that his best work was done at UCLA as a student and then, later, at Amherst where he was teaching. His choreography then, he says, was

> nothing groundbreaking, nothing revolutionary, but really good solid work. But [after awhile,] I no longer had the passion or interest. And above all, the only thing that interested me was the process. The performance, seeing it onstage, touring, and having a company had no interest. I had been through it. I had also realized—the narcissism of the field began to grind on me, the self-involvement of the people, the limited interest most of them had—the fact that they didn't read papers and couldn't care. . . .

As he has matured, Kedelsky's interests have come to encompass more than dance and to embrace, as he says, "the broader cultural area, the cross-cultural exchange of ideas, . . . and the question of how people look at each other." During the summer of 1987, he was offered the opportunity to curate an evening of "The Dance and Music of Africa" for Jacob's Pillow, a summer dance festival in New England. The resulting program was a sampler of groups, each hailing from a different region of Africa. He organized the show around the same philosophical concerns which guided his presentation of the Australian Aboriginal performers in the early 1980s. Before the Jacob's Pillow program, Debra Cash described Kedelsky for *The Boston Globe* and discussed how he conceived his role:

> Spider Kedelsky is a wiry man with black-rimmed glasses who calls himself "an outside cultural broker. My job," explained Kedelsky, who has been an associate professor in the departments of theater and dance at Amherst College, "is to find a way of presenting traditional art in a way that does not compromise the artists or their communities, but makes it comfortable and edifying for audiences." (1987)

Today, at forty-five, Kedelsky is seeking a position where he can expand into an exploration of these concerns, presenting and producing work which addresses a broad cultural viewpoint. He is extremely articulate and incisive. The diversity of his background and wide-ranging interests separate him from many dance artists and perhaps make it inevitable that he would find the studio-based dancers' life too limited. Perhaps, like David White, Kedelsky is an example of why the leadership in the dance field is concentrated among men: a late-starter, bringing other interests and skills to the field, absorbing what there is to be learned, and then marrying that knowledge with other areas of inquiry and expertise. White, of course, is in a position where he can bring his ideas to fruition. At present, Kedelsky has only the ideas.

He believes that dance has a difficult time legitimizing itself in the academic world and/or achieving legitimacy through literature and documentation because dance, more than any other art, is primarily concerned with the act of doing. For this reason, it is hard to discuss. It has its own kind of thinking which does not easily translate to other modes of communication, making it difficult to comprehend on a theoretical level. In our culture today, he says, dance has lost its reason for being; the impulse to dance has become irrevocably changed. In other cultures, according to Kedelsky, dance is

> inextricably tied into social and ritual activities. Those activities have become really reduced in our society, to the point where dance becomes a kind of decorative or recreational form.

The result is an art without potency and importance as a cultural force.

Kedelsky, who, as a consultant for the NEA, sees a wide variety of dance, has strong opinions about the choreography being done today:

> The '60s were much more exciting. ... I don't see the kind of experimentation ... the kind of risk taking, and ... I see ... what's a little frightening sometimes, with this complete emphasis on almost a kind of ... aesthetic aerobics. Like Stephen Petronio, I mean, the movement is spectacular, the dancers are just the best, but after about twenty minutes, I just say to myself ... "Oh, forget this. I mean, what is this man saying?" There has to be more to life than just sheer physical—I want content. I want some passion. I want more intellect. I want something about relationships. I want something more than bodies just furiously driving around. And I understand that's about youth ... but ... I see Molissa Fenley and she's doing the same thing she was doing ten years ago. . . .

And then he considers the context for much of this work. "It speaks of the age," he says. "It's an empty age."

A Summing Up

The four voices offered here do not present a unified view, and in fact, seem to raise as many questions as they answer. What they accomplish, however, is an acknowledgment of the individuality, the singularity of the struggles which shape modern dance as an art. In giving a human shape and form to the gradually evolving field, cultural changes are revealed as forces within individual lives and expressed through the common concerns which focus artists' work. At the most basic level, these are four individual responses to the shared problems of context, economics, creativity, and age.

The stories illustrate the ascendency of funding as a force which has shaped the organizations and institutions constituting the professional field of dance, as well as the lives of those whose work forms the art itself. Funding guidelines and the necessity of showing growth in each year-end statement affected the goals adopted by artists in the 1970s and gradually funding awards became hallmarks of acceptable work. These four each began their own companies in the 1970s and all organized themselves into not-for-profit corporations with expanding budgets established as the primary measure of success. In addition, they each had to cope with the need for a working board of directors and for professional management. These are changes which affect the lives of most dance artists today.

Keen and Posin, both dancers from childhood, have, throughout their lives, seen New York City as the commercial and artistic center of the dance world, the source of work and community. In spite of continuing difficulties in finding balance, security and satisfaction, they hold fast to the model of the New York artist with which they began. Though the culture has changed, and with it, the rules for success and the stakes, both women look to themselves to understand and improve their lives and careers. They cite naivete as a personal flaw and speak of their interest in dancing as an inadequate preparation for survival in the field today.

Kedelsky, on the other hand, used dance as a means of exploring and understanding the world. Now, as a mature artist and person, he too is seeking a place for himself and a means of putting his ideas and skills to work, though in a different arena. His challenge is to move from the freelance, independent world of the artist/teacher to the more institutionalized, established, bureaucratic levels of the field in order to achieve a role which will allow him to make use of the broad cultural perspective he has developed over the years.

There seems a general acknowledgment within the field that in the 1980s an institutional affiliation is more and more necessary for achievement and impact on any sort of scale. This kind of thinking is a shift from the thought of the 1960s and 1970s, when artists felt more powerful and more important within the culture, and the key to this shift seems to be an economic one. Even Twyla Tharp, cited by both Posin and Keen as the model of financial savvy and success, has, at this writing, joined the American Ballet Theater as resident choreographer, disbanding her own company. On January 31, 1989, she was quoted in the *Wall Street Journal* as saying, "Small companies have become economically unworkable. Joining ABT is an attempt to find a solution to the problem" (Harris, p. A-16). Coming from Tharp, a widely accepted artist who has achieved both popular and critical acclaim, a statement like this would seem to set out a new definition of the possibilities within the field.

Small dance businesses still endure, however, and Jeff James speaks to that way of life, though even she has now aligned her organization with a national network. James found herself working in a city where she had to create her own opportunities, and where it was still possible to do so. She has not achieved national fame in the sense of the other three because she has not been working within range of the national media. Within her region, however, James has built a solid reputation while doing work which affords her the satisfaction of knowing that she has made a difference.

All four of these artists mention the fun and pleasure involved in dancing and note a lack of response from the broad American public. Perhaps, as Kedelsky says, dance really is about the doing of it, an attitude which has been largely lost in the spectator culture of the United States today.

Keen, Posin, and Kedelsky all describe dance as being lost and as seeking a renewed purpose and identity in the modern world. None question the role of major federal funding, a force which appeared and matured during their lifetimes. As recipients of Endowment and foundation support, they express an attitude that is understandably one of appreciation. It seems possible, however, that the loss of purpose felt by the field can be traced, in part, to NEA efforts to increase audiences, thereby expanding activity and opportunity and assisting the evolution of dance into business. The net effect of this has been one of giving modern dance economic goals, thus making the field compatible with the culture, while robbing it of its original counter-cultural stance.

Moreover, over the years, funders have said to artists, not only "You need a manager and we'll help pay for it," but "If you don't get a manager, we won't fund you" (Dunn, 1991, p.11). The professionalism of management has served to separate the administration from the artistic life of companies, allowing artists to retreat to the studio, isolating themselves from the community. Additionally, while most artists have welcomed administrative help, making it a requirement seems to imply that perhaps artists cannot take care of themselves. When the day to day decisions of management are completely given over to professionals, artists easily lose touch with the business end of the work, and as a result, forego having a voice in directing the course of the organization. In this way, conflicts between artistic and business values are sometimes not even recognized, allowing organizations to evolve and expand, independent of the artistic vision with which they began. At the same time, without the community contact which management requires, choreographers and dancers often work in their own world without a sense of context or connection to the society at large.

When viewed as something to sell, dance seems to demand most those skills which catch the eye, focusing dance artists on production and technique. Though the culture rewards and reinforces this approach to dance in the short term, the overspecialization which necessarily follows a lifetime of technique classes is a long-term cost, resulting in limitations in other areas of life and art. As Kathryn Posin says, the field has changed in twenty-five years, and has lost the sense of "value in what we are doing." Perhaps it is time to acknowledge these effects and rethink the way dance students are prepared, seeking a meaningful connection with the culture and the means of rediscovering that sense of value.

IV

Higher Education and the Professional Dance World

Introduction

The influence of the NEA on dance is less direct in higher education than in the professional world. It can be seen most clearly in a growing interest in technique and in establishing standards of excellence within college dance programs. Both dancers and choreographers today find themselves swept up in the culture-wide worship of success, spectacle, and mastery. In a sense, Western dance has always held those qualities to be important and has tailored its training programs to suit its values. For a time, however, it seemed that with the work of H'Doubler, Graham, Sokolow, and others, individualism and democratic thought would have an influence on the art and on the lives of dancers. But traditional ways continue to exert a profound influence on standards within the field, on methods of training, and on priorities within dancers' lives. These, in combination with the influence of the market and the broadening of the audience, have contributed to a marked change in the way modern dance views itself and its possibilities.

It is widely conceded that higher education in the United States in general has been narrowing and focusing on job or career oriented skills while neglecting the development of a broad cultural perspective; this is no doubt related to the growing emphasis on quantitative measurement throughout American society. The dance field lends itself easily to such a technical orientation. Young dancers are, by and large, athletes, hungry to move and increase their physical mastery, while dance teachers, who tend to rate themselves according to how professionally successful their students become, often concentrate on training the dancer rather than educating the person. Moreover, as dance grows increasingly competitive, there is diminishing incentive or rationale within the field for doing things differently.

The resulting lack of balance which typifies the education of many professionally-oriented dance students today creates problems in individual lives and in interaction within the field. Examples can be found in the hierarchical relations typical of most schools and companies, the passivity exhibited by many dancers with regard to events outside the dance studio, and an art with a tenuous connection with the world at large. Rigorous, balanced dance education is an idea which has not been taken seriously by the field. Moreover, training procedures exaggerate the importance of the technical aspect of dance, leaving aside philosophical, ideological, and even aesthetic impulses.

The Endowment itself notes, in its *Five-Year Planning Document 1990–94*, that professional schools are not preparing students for long-term artistic growth as opposed to simply preparing them for the first years of employment, and that many qualified artists are not attracted to teaching. Special mention is made of dancers' problems with career transitions, and the question of dance training is said to be under study by the Dance Program and Panel (p. 25).

Many of the concerns covered in the *Planning Document* relate to the shift to large-scale marketing within the dance world, the rapid rise of "professionalism" in dance, and the accelerating competition within the field for jobs, audiences, and visibility. Over the past twenty-five years, technical expertise has become increasingly important for modern dancers, encouraged by the culture's interest in spectacle, and by the art's new association with the ethics of postmodern culture. Technique sells. For a dancer, this often means a trade-off between getting the kind of training which will result in a secure job with a successful company or getting an education which will allow for the development of judgment, creativity, and the use of language.

At the heart of this issue are two arguments: one for dance training and career enhancement, the other for the development of humanistic elements within the person who is the dancer. The latter point of view reminds us that dancers are human beings, citizens with the need to reflect on the world and act responsibly to it and within it, as well as artists who will benefit from acquiring an understanding of the culture. The former sees dancers as physical beings and would characterize dance programs as training grounds for the professional dance world.

From the beginning, the relationship of university dance programs to the professional field has been a dynamic one. In the early 1900s, dance was brought into the academic setting as an integrated part of the curriculum, with the aim of encouraging uniqueness and balance within each student. Throughout the 1930s, 1940s, and 1950s, although academic dance programs helped spread the word about the new modern dance and provided dance artists with performance opportunities, the goals of the profession were essentially different from those of the university, breeding a deep mutual suspicion. However, changes in American society since the 1960s, combined with policies of the NEA, have caused a rearrangement in the relationship of modern dance to the university. University administrators have become more interested in programs which teach professional excellence, and academic dance programs have begun to adopt the values and goals of professional training schools. These ideas are reflected in the standards set forth by the National Association of Schools of Dance, discussed later in this chapter.

The focus of dance and dancers has been restricted by this shift, tending to set the art apart from American society. Those with a narrow perspective are effectively isolated within their particular realm of expertise. As a result, dance has been cut out of the discourse of world affairs, relegated to the periphery, not implicated or even consulted in rethinking the culture. In fact, the reverse seems true: The culture has begun reshaping dance, including the way in which oncoming generations are trained.

Modern Dance and the University

The University of Wisconsin offered its first dance courses in 1919, and in 1926 established the first dance degree program in the nation (Kraus & Chapman, 1981, p. 157). The Wisconsin Idea was based on the work of Margaret H'Doubler, who began her career in the physical education department at the university. In 1916, Blanche Trilling, the head of that department, asked H'Doubler to research the possibilities of including dance in the curriculum. H'Doubler spent a year in New York City, attending performances, studying movement, and doing graduate work at Teachers College with Gertrude Colby and Bird Larson. Then she returned to Wisconsin where, over time, she devised a system of teaching dance in physical education classes (Ruyter, 1979, p. 117).

H'Doubler's approach was widely accepted and became the standard method of dance training in higher education for many years to come. It was a system designed for training dance teachers. H'Doubler drew on the work of John Dewey, who believed that schools should prepare students to live effectively and harmoniously in the world and to make the world a better place. In his view, education was training for democracy. Ruyter quotes Dewey as saying that in a democracy, "the conventional type of education which trains children to docility and obedience, to the careful performance of imposed tasks because they are imposed" was out of place, because it did not prepare one for the responsibility of self-government (p. 101). H'Doubler took these ideas and searched for a means of integrating them with dance training, to devise a method less formal, artificial, and authoritarian than the traditional system. In 1925, according to Ruyter, H'Doubler described the new form of dancing which she and others were developing as "primarily democratic," going on to say:

> It serves all the ends of education—it helps to develop the body, to cultivate the love and appreciation of beauty, to stimulate the imagination and challenge the intellect, to deepen and refine the emotional life, and to broaden the social capabilities of the individual that he may at once profit from and serve the greater world without. (p. 102)

Philosophically, H'Doubler considered the expressive aspect of dance central to life, and technique a necessary component of the form because it provides the tools for flexibility, strength, and control. Although she valued musical training as an important part of dance, her approach was based in science, because she believed that teachers must know how the body works. "Natural" was the word H'Doubler herself used to describe the system, and in regard to her knowledge of contemporary science and her concern with doing what is healthy and normal for a body to do, the term applies. But because she did believe in an acquired technique, the work was not natural in the sense of other dancers of her time, notably, Isadora Duncan. In addition, Ruyter writes:

> There can be no doubt about where H'Doubler stood on the question of artistic standards as against educational goals. She would never have sacrificed the one for the other. Nevertheless, her system was rigorous and demanding—not at the expense of educational goals, but in the interest of them. (p. 121)

During the early 1930s, the University of Wisconsin program became the model for physical education-based dance departments throughout the United States (Kraus & Chapman, p. 257). From the beginning these departments provided shelter and subsistence for modern dance as it developed, not only through their classes, but also through the performances they sponsored during the 1930s, 1940s, and 1950s. Modern dance has by now loosened its close alliance with physical education in the university, along with the emphasis on dance as a means of educating for democracy. Dance in the 1990s has become more diversified, and is sometimes allied with theater or music. Because of its growth since the early days, it has gained a good deal of autonomy as a discipline. At the time, however, the partnership with physical education ensured the survival of the form during a period when, according to Don McDonagh, modern dance "could not afford to take a longer-term look at its ultimate goals" (1973, p. 112). He suggests that because early modern dancers were serious minded, the popular theater was closed to them, and the university offered an alternate route to survival. In his view, the alliance was a mixed blessing, however, and affected the development of modern dance as an art:

> No matter how hard college dance . . . departments try, they never manage to capture a thoroughly professional air or level of performance. At times, their utter disdain for the practical necessities occasioned by commercial pressures produces admirable results that can be attained in no other manner, and there is no question that modern dance as it developed would not have been possible without the generous assistance of the universities and colleges. But it is

also likely that, had the dance come of age outside the academy, it would not have grown up with such a pedagogical attitude toward developing its audience—the attitude, in a sense, of a teacher who will not go out of his way to popularize a course or advertise it in any manner that might be construed unfavorably as implying enjoyment. In the eyes of the educational world, fun meant a lack of seriousness. Modern dance found it hard to laugh, and this was one reason it was exceptionally difficult to fill a hall outside of colleges. (McDonagh, 1973, p. 111)

Then, assuming McDonagh is right, the heritage of modern dance stems from a lack of concern with commercial values, combined with an involvement in social issues. This is the heart of an important point: Modern dance began and developed as a form which made no concessions to its audience. As an art, it was utterly creator-oriented, and it is the loss of this point of view which writers like Lipman and Joyce decry (see Chapter II). The postmodern age has brought with it a commercial consciousness, making accessibility a virtue. There is no longer a moral high ground in austerity and depth of meaning. Now, the socially acceptable position for artists lies in making an effort to share, in reaching out, as exemplified in Chapter II by Bill T. Jones's defense of his decision to make accessible work by citing his belief in socialism.

Professionalism in Academia

Because university dance programs traditionally required creative and/or scientific work and theoretical study, while sometimes downplaying the importance of technical training, they have tended to attract and develop a dancer more interested in ideas and individual expression than those trained in professional studios. Before 1970, university dance students normally went on to become the dancer/teachers or dancer/scholars of the field, with only a small percentage making a career of performing. Within the field, it is widely held that it takes ten years of training to make a dancer. The lack of emphasis on technique in the academic curriculum allowed universities and colleges to graduate students in four years, though many were, at that point, not employable as professional dancers.

Thus, over time, in spite of their mutual dependence, a schism developed between the academic dance world and the professional field about the role of the university as a training ground, reflecting what has been a deep divergence in values. The question is whether one is trying to educate the person or train the dancer—to teach skills or build inner resources. Cannot both points of view operate and carry influence within the same system? So far, there has not been much interest in developing such a model.

In their discussion of dance and the goals of contemporary education, Kraus and Chapman mention that within colleges and universities, by the late 1950s the stress on life adjustment goals had gone out of style. They say that similarly, the pursuit of dance as an art was also difficult at this time because of the furor following the first Russian Sputnik. With

> the disclosure of the advanced level of Soviet education in mathematics, science, and engineering, there was a "crash" program of strengthening these areas of education. By default, the arts necessarily received less support and attention. (1981, p. 262)

By the end of the 1980s, attitudes within the academic dance setting had shifted again, this time toward a striving for credibility among dance professionals. In an effort to bring the values of the field more to the fore, dance faculties adopted professional equivalencies to academic degrees, allowing for the increased hiring of performing artists as teachers. Additionally, some have encouraged older dancers to return to school by permitting the transformation of professional career experiences into academic credit. Since the mid-1960s, the number of dance curricula in American colleges and universities has grown steadily, particularly in programs which emphasize the performing arts. The trend has been to move away from an administrative base in physical education, becoming either an independent dance department or program, or part of a department or school concerned with other performing arts, such as music or theater (Kraus & Chapman, 1981, p. 292).

Despite the fact that there has been little direct interaction between the NEA and university dance programs, it is possible to see the NEA as an active force in academia. The growth in numbers and in professional orientation described above coincides with the rapid rise in the number of modern dance companies in the United States during the 1970s. Leila Sussman (1984) provides statistics which show that 28 modern dance groups listed themselves in the *Dance Magazine Annual* in 1958. In 1970 there were 102 listed and in 1980, 289. Sussman credits the support of the NEA for this boom (p. 24), as does MacNeil Lowry (1978, p. 22–23).

In addition, Sussman provides figures which show that 60% of the new modern dance companies founded during the 1970s were based outside New York City, probably a reflection of NEA policies as well. No doubt, the rise in the number of companies around the United States stimulated interest in dance among students and increased the demand for classes. In response, dance programs set about preparing students for dance jobs—jobs made available through funding of companies and the presenters who produce their work. Doubtless, also, as dance programs expanded, the increase in college educated dance graduates spurred the rise of small companies throughout the United States. Interest in performance as a profession grew as the field seemed to offer opportunity.

One result of this expansion has been a move to institutionalize professional training standards within colleges and universities. In 1981, representatives from educational dance programs met in Washington, DC to consider the establishment of an accreditation association for educational programs in dance. As a result of that meeting, the National Association of Schools of Dance was formed. Forty-eight institutions became charter members: ten professional dance training organizations and thirty-eight colleges and universities.

NASD describes its function as one of finding

> ways of clarifying and maintaining standards in dance through the responsible education of dancers. By means of accreditation, it can encourage those institutions that consistently give students a sound basis for significant future accomplishments in dance. (*NASD Brochure Describing Functions of the Association*, p. 2)

Membership is based on criteria such as curriculum, admission policies, sequencing of classes, length of time in operation, faculty qualifications, facilities and equipment, advertising, financial policies, and student access to libraries. Standards and guidelines are described as having evolved from a synthesis of thought about professional training in dance, and are to be used as part of the peer review process of accreditation, rather than as rules and regulations. According to NASD literature, standards for admission are meant to provide the basis for dialogue within an institution as the self-study (which is necessary for application) is being developed, and then between an institution and the Association (during the period of evaluation), and finally, between the Association and the general public.

Rona Sande, director of the Dance Division at the University of California at Santa Barbara, was one of the dance educators who formulated these standards. Sande says that the NASD has, in a real sense, given university dance departments permission to do what many now want to do anyway: require an intensive studio component within their programs. Additionally, she says, accreditation has helped legitimize dance programs within the university community, particularly among administrators with budgetary and discretionary powers.

The Association has three categories of accredited membership. (The NASD brochure describes the categories as follows: "Division I includes schools and institutions whose predominant purpose and enrollment are in the development of the technical skills and artistry requisite for a career as a dance professional. Programs in Division I may or may not lead to a professional certificate or diploma. Division II membership includes schools and departments whose predominant purpose and enrollment are in the development of technical skills and artistry requisite for a career as a dance professional and who offer one or more academic degrees. Division III membership includes schools and departments whose purpose and enrollment are in quality education in dance as a curricular major within a general liberal arts program and/ or as the basis of scholarly study.")

Division I is for dance schools and studios wanting legitimation in the eyes of the profession and the public, and Divisions II and III are for college and university departments seeking professional credibility. The separation between Divisions II and III marks the difference between a "professional" degree and a "liberal arts" degree. The Associate of Fine Arts and the Bachelor of Fine Arts degrees are both included in Division II and both "require that at least 65% of the course credit be in studio work and related areas" (*NASD Handbook 1988–89*, p. 40). This describes a strongly focused course of study, narrowed to the development of technical skills and dance artistry, in essence, a vocational degree.

The liberal arts degrees are called Associate of Arts or Science and Bachelor of Arts or Science with a major in dance. These degrees usually require that one-third to one-half the total course credit be in dance. NASD describes Division III as including "schools and departments whose predominant purpose and enrollment are in quality education in dance" (*NASD Brochure*, p. 3), a telling distinction from the BFA (Division II) which has as "its primary emphasis ... the development of skills, concepts and sensibilities essential to the dance professional" (*NASD Handbook*, p. 41). The difference between Division II and Division III points to the dissimilarity in emphasis between educating dancers as people and educating dancers for dance. It also suggests an issue which is becoming more important within the dance world itself: What is the relationship between intensive technical training and intellectual, physical, and emotional development? Does technical training produce technical thinkers? Can educators reconcile the demand from the field for excellence in technique with the simultaneous demand for choreographers who have both skill and vision?

The Education and Training of Dancers

The implication is best framed as a question: With its focus on training, the term used to describe a dancer's concentration on technique and production, does current dance education deny students balance? Can a lack of verbal confidence be attributed to years of intensive physical discipline? How is the passive acceptance, among dancers, of professional situations which are sometimes inhumane explained, and the lack of power many feel in response to press coverage, the political dance establishment, or in simply being able to speak intelligently about the field?

Among many dancers, there is a notable lack of relationship with the world outside the dance studio. In fact, dancers often accept a lack of general power within society in exchange for the very personal sense of power that comes from having strong physical skills. This trade-off has disturbing implications. The original modern dancers, the thinkers who pioneered the field, were not technicians. They did not grow up in dance studios. Isadora Duncan and Ruth St. Denis were largely self-taught (Page, 1984, p. vii). Both trained sporadically in assorted styles ranging from Delsartian interpretations to ballroom dance, acrobatic tricks, and a brief introduction to ballet (Ruyter, 1979).

Throughout the past century, many of the artists considered leaders in modern dance, the innovators, the more creative minds, were not people who trained intensively as children. Doris Humphrey did start dancing at the age of eight (Humphrey, 1966, p. 17), but Martha Graham waited, because of parental opposition, until she was twenty-two to begin her studies (McDonagh, 1976, p. 52). Paul Taylor got "a flash, or whatever it is ... telling me that I'm to become a dancer—not any old dancer, but one of the best" (Taylor, 1987, p. 26), when he was a sophomore in college with no previous experience. Though Merce Cunningham has had a lifelong interest in theater and began intermittent childhood study at the age of eight, he came to the study of modern dance during his college years (Cunningham, 1985, p. 33).

Erick Hawkins began studying dance after college graduation (McDonagh, 1976, p. 297), and Jose Limon, who thought he would be a painter, came to his first dance classes at the age of twenty (Gadan & Maillard, 1959, p. 214). Alwin Nikolais initiated his training at the Bennington College School of Dance as a young man (Gadan & Maillard, p. 242), and Alvin Ailey started studying with Lester Horton while in his teens (Mazo, 1984, p. 23). Yvonne Rainer says she began studying dance in earnest in 1959, when she was twenty-five (Rainer, 1974, p.5).

These experiences raise a number of issues on the broad question of how people learn to dance. Is there a relationship between technical training and creativity and leadership? As bodies are trained to be disciplined and obedient instruments, skilled at following directions, accustomed to taking correction, working silently to become a vehicle for another person's ideas, are minds trained in the same way? These concerns bear thoughtful examination. Discipline and obedience are high on the list of values we instill in dance students, and they are, on the whole, not the makings of creative leadership and innovation. When, in today's culture, dance classes are part of growing up for many young girls, are they, in fact, put at a disadvantage in terms of development? Are they given movement and technical skills while sacrificing the development of language and social skills?

What would Yvonne Rainer's work have been like had she studied dance for ten years before arriving in New York? As it was, at twenty-five she had no tradition to uphold. And though she was an earnest student, the realization that she would never fit the mold of "dancer" in this society gave her an ambivalence which developed into a radical response, an adversarial posture in regard to the dance establishment (Chin, 1975). "The choices in my work are predicated on my own peculiar resources ... and also on an ongoing argument with, love of, and contempt for dancing " (Rainer, p. 71), she said, and in this context, the extraordinary directions she pursued make clear sense.

> I suspected that I would never be "good enough" to dance
> in an official company. Although I was becoming more pro-

ficient in conventional technical matters, the chunky construction of my body and my lack of natural litheness did not fit the popular image of the female dancer. (Chin, p. 51)

So she made work which defied that image. More important, she was not so identified with dance that she could not defy it. Because she had a broad background to bring to it, her work was not about trying to fit in.

The conflict between the broad education needed for personal growth and the intensive training required for professional excellence is obvious. Creativity is believed to be fostered when students are encouraged to exhibit individuality and to make their own choices rather than being regimented by imposed restraints or required conformity. Kraus and Chapman (p. 264) state that most dance educators believe their position in education is strengthened by a growing recognition of the need for educational experiences which will provide a sense of personal involvement, to help students become aware of their uniqueness and become capable of making meaningful judgments within all areas of life. It is ironic that dance is known to bring these experiences to a general curriculum while the same considerations are not reflected in the way professionally oriented dance students are being taught.

In its listing in the *88/89 Dancemagazine College Guide*, the University of California at Santa Barbara, a public, state-supported university, makes clear the differences between the two degrees offered by its dance department:

> The BFA degree is oriented toward training the dance student for a professional career in performance and/or choreography and the curriculum is centered around studio courses and related theatrical experiences. The BA degree is a less structured program and allows time for students to pursue course work that could lead to alternate careers. ... (p. 87)

The narrowing of focus which is part of a professionally-oriented dance program in fact cuts out the social and philosophical grounding needed to understand the world and form a response to it, no doubt affecting both art and lives in the long run. A point of view, necessary to the development of one's own voice as an artist, needs cultivation and stimulation, exposure to ideas, and faith in one's own ability to know truth.

Choreographer Liz Lerman provides a telling example of the process. She grew up with an on again-off again desire to dance. As a student, her frustration with dancing stemmed from the insular experience of the dance studio and its lack of pertinence to her life: "I wanted dancing to be a major part of my life, reflecting my primary concerns. I wanted it to be humane, a humane experience" (Kriegsman, 1987, p. G7). Lerman points to a turning point, a major growth period at Bennington College, which happened not in the dance department, but with an American history teacher: "I learned how to trust myself, how to find my own ideas apart from received ones, and how to organize them" (Kriegsman, p. G7). As she matured, she oriented her work in dance away from the accepted postmodern aesthetic and toward life, community, and culture. Lerman's work has been described as connected

> directly with a tradition of humanist dance whose exponents have included Doris Humphrey, Charles Weidman, Lester Horton, Martha Graham, Hanya Holm, Anna Sokolow, Alvin Ailey and Anna Halprin, among others. (Kriegsman, 1987, p. G7)

And in 1991 David White of New York's Dance Theater Workshop, named Lerman when asked which dancer/choreographer, in his opinion, best reflects the times. Saying that for him, "The *meat* [emphasis his] of the matter is the ideas we raise as essential challenges to a dangerous complacency that has come to characterize our public society and private lives," he cited Lerman's "revelatory social thinking applied to the practice of making dances while building community" as putting her ahead of the field (Eginton, 1991, p.11).

John Gamble, head of the University of North Carolina-Greensboro Dance Department affirms the importance of the kind of learning experience Lerman had at Bennington. He describes the key to creative artistry as "the power to have opinions" (personal communication, 1988), and suggests that today's technically-based BFA degree is less likely to produce artists with this kind of confidence because of its stress on building skills rather than on developing a world view.

However, in Gamble's opinion, the scientifically-based body awareness classes taught in university physical education/dance departments were not much better. H'Doubler's response to the restrictions of ballet training was only a switch from one limited viewpoint to another, and the BFA is the latest development in this sequence. None of these approaches provide the dance student with connections to the world outside the studio. The physical education emphasis is now on the wane, and according to Gamble, where dance is departmentalized, the BFA degree tends to be in place. It is left to the BA degree, often housed in liberal arts colleges, to provide balance. Historic examples have been the dance program at Bennington and that at Sarah Lawrence College.

In the current push for technical excellence, however, the liberal arts have been discounted by the professional dance world. Even an educator like Gamble, holding broad-based ideas about learning, has felt that participation in an organization such as NASD is valuable. He is in the process of revising the dance program at UNCG to fall in line with NASD standards. In his view, the 65% requirement can be arranged to fit one's conception of what a dance professional needs and might include art history, cultural literacy, and philosophy components if that is what one considers important. (In most BFA and many MFA programs, knowledge in these areas is not held necessary to artistic growth, or not important enough, at least, to displace technique or production classes within the curriculum.)

Gamble describes the Association as an opportunity to be part of an important network formed from the professional and academic worlds, an opportunity to bridge misunderstandings and build liaisons. More concretely, meetings offer the chance to discuss curriculum, to find out how other schools are doing things, and to place students in jobs. In addition, Gamble echoes Sande's assertion that accreditation gives muscle to a dance program when addressing university administration.

The Conservatory Tradition

Although the 65% studio-related course of study mandated for the BFA within the university can be narrow and limiting, the concentration of the conservatory is even more extreme. No matter how excellent the dancer, without a broad-based educational background he or she is vulnerable and relatively powerless in the world outside the studio.

The North Carolina School of the Arts was established by an act of the North Carolina Legislature in 1963. It is open by audition to high school and college students throughout the nation. A BFA in dance is offered, an arts diploma for those not taking a full academic load, and a high school diploma for younger students. Professional training constitutes the major emphasis in the course of study (Kraus & Chapman, p. 290), and a job in the arts, rather than graduation, is the emphasis of the teaching and training process (Catanoso, 1988, p. A12).

On October 30, 1988, the *Greensboro News and Record* featured an article on the School of the Arts which discussed the standards at the school and the teaching approach. Though not all those quoted here were talking about dance, analogies can be clearly drawn. The school selects its 753 students both by audition and on the basis of academic record. "But we don't kid ourselves," says Bill Tribby, dean of general studies. "Nobody comes here with the intent of being an English major" (Steadman, p. H5). Former dean Robert Lindgren seems to sum up school policy with the remark that "The elitist attitude, of which we have been so often accused, is something I share as well. Not everyone who wants to become a dancer can become one" (Horosko, 1988, p. 69).

Training at the school is competitive and exclusionary, based on fulfilling predetermined standards of performance, following directions, and satisfying externally imposed notions of excellence. Ballet instructor Melissa Hayden, a former dancer with George Balanchine, is quoted as telling a class, "You don't have to believe me ... you don't have to trust me. ... You only have to do what I ask. ... We don't want nice little girls; we want good dancers" (Steadman, 1988, p. H5). "Tense" is how an eighteen-year-old dance major describes the school. "This school is tense because it is *intense*. When I drive back for each term, I feel it" (p. H5).

Cranford Johnson, dean of student affairs, says that students must deal with "the stress of a heavy program, time pressures and high expectations ... they tend to do well or they don't stay long. They are not invited back" (p. H5). Throughout Steadman's article, mention is made of pressure in training, justified by the staff as a means of preparing students for the competition and difficulties of the professional world. "We run our curriculum with a sense of that future competition," states an art instructor. An acting teacher adds, "That's what the whole training is about—pressure ... otherwise we would be encouraging people to enter an area where they didn't qualify." Allen Rust, the drama dean, sums it up: "Our goal is to have people working ... it's not just an art when you get out of here; it's a business" (p. H5).

In an essay addressing problems involved with teaching dance, Julia Buckroyd points out that these teaching methods fly in the face of current educational theory. Her response to this kind of educational atmosphere is a rebuttal of the traditional dance class:

> The task of the teacher is not to fill the empty vessel of the
> student out of her fullness, but rather to stimulate and sup-

port the student's own resources for learning. . . . Such learning not only respects the individuality and worth of the individual but in measurable ways produces better results even as conventionally measured, while at the same time eliciting much greater pleasure in learning and much greater growth in self-confidence and self-esteem in the students. (1988a, p. 647)

Buckroyd goes on to say that she is aware that her ideas are untraditional for dance and she expects that dance teachers will object that, in learning a technique such as Graham or ballet, the teacher must be the source. One cannot learn to dance from a book. As there is a right and wrong, teachers will say that "corrections" are necessary, and since standards of professional dance are inhumanly high, to encourage or praise in more than minimal doses may "induce wholly unrealistic expectations of life as a professional dancer." She replies to these objections by saying:

It is clear that the world is often a very harsh and very unfair place. We prepare our children to function in this difficult world by giving them as much love and security as we know how, believing that from this firm base they will best be able to deal with life's rigors. I think the same about dance students. If the professional dance world is as savage as it is supposed to be, students will deal best with it who are confident and self-assured, rather than demoralized and undermined. . . . As long as we insist on doing all the leading, our students will gladly do the following. But we do them no service by treating them as infants who need spoonfeeding. We keep them in an artificially regressed state. (1988a, p. 649)

Buckroyd stresses that she is not a dancer but a student counselor (at the London Contemporary Dance School), and so can offer no concrete suggestions for new ways of working. But she encourages teachers of dance to do less for their students, to let them take some responsibility for their own learning, to learn from each other, and find the motivations within themselves for committing themselves to dance. Allowing them this kind of personal as well as technical growth should, she says

produce dancers who are more developed as human beings, better able to grapple with whatever difficulties their professional careers pose them. It may also nurture dancers capable of developing dance as an art. From all that I hear dancers are technically able as never before, while the art languishes way behind their technical capacity. (1988a, p. 649)

Buckroyd's is a lonely voice in a field consumed by the idea that dance is about technique. The Juilliard School in New York City is another example of a conservatory which trains musicians, dancers, and drama students. In the *Stern's Performing Arts Directory 1989*, it advertises itself as providing

> Training for the professional dancer. Curriculum includes major study in ballet and modern dance techniques, repertory and performance, dance composition, dance notation, dance history, anatomy for dancers, and studies in music—Programs leading to a diploma or Bachelor of Fine Arts degree. (p. D-85)

Judith Kogan discusses the intensity of student life at Juilliard in her book *Nothing But the Best* (1987). Her writing focuses on the training of musicians, but the analogy is clear when she says that at Juilliard, ability and technique are loosely equated and that, in her experience, the never-ending focus on technical skill can blind one to music itself. "In some ways," she says, "music is appreciated not as something beautiful but as a tool of commerce" (p. 48). She writes of how, under the constant stress on perfection, young performers come to define themselves by how well they perform and, inevitably, on the basis of how well others think they perform (p. 142).

As a teenager, Jefferson James attended Juilliard for two years, from 1961–1963. "My primary interest," she said in a 1988 interview, "was in dance —in developing technique, and that's what interested me about Juilliard." Juilliard admits students through a system of auditions. At the time, James said, she was judged on technique and performance, and given a physical examination to determine any problems which might interfere with her development. The experiences she had as a dancer at Juilliard twenty-five years ago echo much of what Kogan writes about the music school. James found the technical training extremely challenging, but there was little emphasis on growth in other areas.

> They really weren't interested in choreography or in developing that side, or certainly not in admitting that kind of talent. They wanted people they could form. ... They figured that [composition class] was part of your education, and they

had a notation course, and Lulu Sweigard was there to teach a ... body awareness sort of class, ... so they realized there were other things that you needed to know, but they weren't teaching that at that time, or any other time, that I can see. ...

Academics and creative work were taught as an adjunct to technique. Though interesting, according to James, they were "not a priority."

Juilliard was a wonderful training ground for technique and really learning about the field. ... There was much less emphasis on choreography, although Lucas Hoving was there and, of course, Louis Horst was there. Louis Horst was very distant from the students. He was there primarily as a disciplinarian. He was not a nurturing sort of choreographic teacher. He had his rules and you either followed them or were chastised. It was one way of teaching us all about form, which, again, was very good discipline, but it certainly wasn't a nurturing atmosphere.

As at the North Carolina School of the Arts, for those talented enough to be admitted, training at Juilliard is seen as a socialization process for the field. Along with striving for mastery, students are exposed to commonly accepted values and methods of the professional world. According to James, the experience was not always positive:

I was really interested in being a dancer and that occupied most of my time at Juilliard. ... I learned a lot of things besides dance, and some of them were sort of frightening for a kid from Alexandria, Virginia ... being around people who were very talented and very frustrated and very unhappy already ... fellow students at Juilliard—a lot of disillusionment ... already, about the field. ...

Though the school offered a professional and technical challenge, James became disenchanted over time, unhappy with the school politics. She says that the disenchantment was mutual.

While I turned off Juilliard, Juilliard sort of turned off of me, because at the beginning of my second year I had my first knee incident [injury]. ... While they didn't do anything overtly, I think they just [decided] this was a person who was not going to have a career.

At the end of her second year, James left to take classes at Columbia

University and continued her professional training at private studios in New York.

The Influence of Ballet Training on the Training of Modern Dancers

In 1969, Juilliard moved to Lincoln Center, invigorated its dance department, and took the preeminent School of American Ballet into its home (Kogan, p. 6). Though there has been a dialogue between modern dance and ballet since the inception of modern dance in the early years of this century, over the last twenty years, the relationship has grown increasingly friendly. In professional and critical circles, there is talk of a melding of viewpoints.

During the decade of the 1980s, ballet companies began looking to modern choreographers for fresh and interesting new work, and modern dancers now regularly study ballet as a means of building technique. This exchange makes clear the relative strengths of each discipline. It also points up the risk if modern dance continues to embrace ballet training methods without question, a methodology which is held by some to limit overall development. Shona Innes writes that, over years, the held state of the body in ballet can produce a corresponding fixity of the intellect and emotion. According to Innes, this striving within the body for a certain sculpted look with everything in its place creates major distortions in dancers' perceptions of themselves and how they relate to other people, and restricts the development of the intellectual, emotional, and physical range necessary to maturity (1988, p. 39).

On the other side of the coin, there is scant evidence of new choreographic talent emerging from within the ballet world and as a result, more and more frequently, ballet companies have come to rely on modern choreographers for additions to the repertory. These companies can provide modern dance choreographers with opportunities for work on a scale which would be out of reach within the modern dance world. This gives the modern artists visibility, but points up a bias in the dance world, a well established imbalance in the financial resources and influence of both forms, and an inequality which is perpetuated by public policy. In 1985, choreographer Alwin Nikolais described it in the following way:

> There is a new project underway. I hope you have objected to it. It's been going on for some time now. Some of the fund-

giving agencies are giving funds to Modern Dancers to create works for ballet companies. It seems as if I'm down on ballet. No, I am not. I'm just down very much on the unintelligent reasoning between the two techniques. I'll give a realistic case here. There is a lady on the West Coast who is becoming a very fine Modern Dance choreographer. Recently she received funds to choreograph on a ballet company, and the thing turned out very successfully. It was a fine piece. In that piece she used three scrims. Each one must have set the budget back $4,000. There went $12,000. Hopefully her fee was about $10,000. Dancers fees and other expenses caused a total expense of $100,000 minimum that went into the creation of that ballet. I asked this person how much she received from the Endowment to create for her own company. She said $7,000. And yet she was asked to do this ballet which cost ten to twelve times that. So I said, "Don't ever do it again unless you get like support for what you yourself do."(p. 117)

Ballet began its expansion into a national phenomenon in 1959 with the first Ford Foundation grants, which provided regional scholarships to dance students outside New York and San Francisco. A 1963 grant funded an expanded, three-tiered program of assistance: scholarships were awarded to students across the country for study at the School of American Ballet in New York City, and members of the school faculty visited and taught at local and regional schools. Additionally, a project was developed to locate and begin to train talented underprivileged children aged eight to ten. In time, these children would become eligible for scholarships and advanced study (Dunning, 1985, p. 113).

This was the beginning of middle America's acquaintance with professional caliber ballet. Coupled with the celebrated defections of three virtuosic Russian dancers, Rudolph Nureyev, Mikhail Baryshnikov, and Natalia Makarova, the training opportunities and media exposure have led to a wide acceptance and appreciation among the general public for the ballet ethic of technical mastery. This, in turn, has influenced the thinking of choreographers and educators wanting to keep up with the demands of public taste. Even modern dancers today feel pressure to achieve excellence in technique, and the influence of ballet is being felt widely in modern training programs, including those in universities. Ballet steps find their way into modern choreography in increasing numbers, as does the balletic sense of ballon and a preference for the long-limbed, thin ballet body.

In a sense, the ballet ethic can be viewed as a systematic removal of individuality by teaching for conformity to an imposed ideal. Interestingly, this phenomenon is beginning to be seen in the original modern dance techniques too, as those techniques are separated from their sources and become codified. In the early years, techniques were invented by the choreographers and dancers who created the original modern dances. Now, in schools across the country, classes are taught by dancers who were not there at the beginning, who have had to understand the styles in a different way. They are not in a position to be innovative. They are teaching "Graham" technique, or "Horton," or "Cunningham." They, like ballet teachers, are passing on a body of knowledge, and in order to do so, they have had to systematize it, make some things right and others wrong, and to create an ideal of time and space based on the style they are teaching.

More important to values within modern dance, however, is the melding of the techniques, made possible by eclectic training and a lack of interest in the philosophical ideals behind each way of working. Most of today's modern dance choreographers have not carried on the early tradition of maintaining a school with their company, so instead of working to learn and understand the style of a particular artist or company, a dance student is given training which stresses versatility, building an all-purpose technique. Ruth Page provides the perspective of many years in dance as she describes the aesthetic changes she has noted:

> The difference between my days as a dancer and today is that all kinds of dancing, especially ballet and modern dance, used to be completely separate. ... Now the styles are so mixed together that it is hard to say where one begins and the other ends. ... It all seems to have produced a blend with an overall sameness that often lacks the stamp of personality, the scent of spirituality, or the passion of a national ethos. That sameness is danced with a perfection of technique we never knew, but quite often, it is artistically boring. (Page, 1984, p. 177)

In American ballet, by far the most significant and authoritative artist has been George Balanchine, and it is largely his influence that is being felt. Robert Lindgren, former dean of the North Carolina School of the Arts, headed Balanchine's school, the School of American Ballet, from 1987–1991. He says that the "Balanchine syllabus and methodology ... has now become American ballet" (Horosko, p. 69). Balanchine's was the ballet company without stars, where the choreography was the important element in performance, and dancers were trained to execute his steps in order to show his dances.

Gelsey Kirkland, a former leading dancer with Balanchine's New York City Ballet, describes the relentless pursuit of technique at SAB and says that through this technical emphasis, dancers were being trained to not interpret a role, and not bring character or individuality to a dance. She quotes former Balanchine dancer Violet Verdy as saying that, in comparison with today, "in the late fifties, the company had dancers with personalities" (1986, p. 83). "Over the years," Kirkland says, "character had been replaced by technique" (p. 83), replaced by an ideal of shape and speed, removing the dance from the person and creating a new standard for perfection. According to Arlene Croce, "Balanchine's classes were his laboratory" (1988, p. 44), and in them, he devised a technique geared to show line and design. "I did not realize the extent to which the limitations of that training were built into the roles and steps themselves," Kirkland writes. "As the steps became disconnected from drama, the roles became disconnected from character" (p. 82).

Dancing ability alone seemed to hold Balanchine's interest in his students. Lincoln Kirstein, cofounder with Balanchine and president of the SAB until 1989, has had much the same view. In response to the school's attempts at providing even ancillary studies, he has said,

> I don't believe in it very much. . . . We are interested in making professional dancers, not in turning out well-rounded gentlefolk. By law we must fulfill the truancy laws. But there is no more reason to teach the kids academic subjects than there is for West Pointers to learn art history. They aren't interested. They're very directed and limited. The idea of a well-rounded ballet student is not important. And it is the temperament of dancers that they don't require a great deal of intellectual stimulation. (Dunning, 1985, p. 203)

Dance writer Jennifer Dunning says that young dancers tend to agree with Kirstein (p. 203). This may be true of many dancers, particularly those who grow up in an atmosphere where role models have no college degrees and/or no interests outside the studio. But rather than being innate to dancers, more likely, this attitude is a matter of socialization. Dancers have traditionally been trained not to speak and question, and, on the whole, have been led to believe that movement study is the only investment they need make. Dunning quotes a young New York City Ballet corps dancer as saying, "Dancers aren't dumb, but I'm afraid most of us have very one-track minds" (p. 203). As a result, the field has a history of low pay, weak unions, and an art which is often seen as being without substance.

Laura Shapiro puts a twist on this argument while discussing the problems ballet companies are having finding star quality American male dancers, and in the process, supports Buckroyd's ideas on educational theory. Shapiro notes that a concentration on classical training in itself does not develop confidence and daring among young boys, a "charismatic masculinity," as she says, and asks whether ballet does not have something to learn from the ethics embedded in modern dance:

> Personality, open-mindedness, a belief in oneself that allows one to take chances—none of these modern-dance traits shows up in any rule book for classical ballet, but maybe they should. What a difference they would make in the ballet studio. ... Surely a dose of modern-dance training would strengthen at least the psychological dimension. ... (1989, p. 63)

Testing and Technique

It is easier to see excellence in technique, to analyze how it works, and certainly easier to teach its rules and guidelines than those of wholeness, balance and artistry. Nationwide, our educational system has become increasingly involved with "accountability," and as a result requires a means of viewing an activity quantitatively to measure success. The arts have not escaped this kind of thinking and consequently, many curricula are organized around the idea that without standards, one cannot gauge and discuss artistry. Technique offers the possibility of measurement that is less subjective than the creative spirit behind choreography.

In the arts, however, the same standards which delineate quality tend to restrict vision. Whenever standards are imposed from the outside to facilitate testing and analysis, there is a risk of codification and a setting up of rules for success. Nevertheless, the National Endowment for the Arts has come very close to advocating the establishment of criteria for quality and value. Long an active supporter of arts in education, the agency is now arguing for nationwide testing and evaluation in the arts in spite of the fact that a standard, testable base of knowledge is required for meaningful statistical testing results (NEA, *Toward Civilization*, 1988, p. 91). "Testing," it says, "is a fact of life in reading, language, mathematics, history, and science. Why not in the arts?"

To its credit, the agency acknowledges the contradiction involved with suggesting a standardized curriculum for a creative and subjective area of learning. It also recognizes that the nature of the arts does not lend itself to traditional standardized multiple choice testing. But although fear is voiced that testing may affect the way the arts are taught, the Endowment has decided to support testing in the arts because of a perceived need to evaluate the effectiveness of various programs and to measure individual progress against curricular goals (raising questions of how to measure this without standardizing curricular goals). Most important, however, the Endowment says, is the idea that what is tested tends to become what the community values. For the NEA, then, testing becomes a means of raising the profile of the arts.

Although Endowment literature is cautionary about how best to do it and notes the importance of testing qualitatively as well as quantitatively, the testing itself seems a dangerous tactic. How can any sort of national effort in evaluation avoid creating national principles of good and bad? A nationwide value system for the arts will enable the Endowment to effect in arts education what it has begun to accomplish in the professional dance world: an adjudicated, administered aesthetic upon which to base objectives for achievement. It seems clear that this will only result in nationally accepted techniques of teaching and evaluating the arts, creating students who are socialized into techniques of producing in order to meet the national standard, as well as audiences who have a standardized response.

The Dancer as a Person

Aside from the limitations a technical emphasis may place on the creative mind, the implications of intensive technical training have to do with time and energy. In dance, a concentrated study of technique during adolescence not only constrains thoughts to predetermined patterns and places the student in a learning situation which is most likely based on following directions and taking corrections, but it limits the time and energy available to broader experience. Kogan has found the same problems in her study of music training at Juilliard. She notes that, among those who survive, eventually, after leaving the rarefied atmosphere of the school, some come to realize that, after all, life is necessary to art.

> Art can't be taught in a classroom or learned in a practice room. Art expresses how the world looks to an artist. Ex-

perience awakens the artist. One need not leave a room to experience life, but one must somehow connect with and respond to the world. (p. 234)

One needs basic technique, she says, but beyond that, artistry is an individual response to life.

Buckroyd regards dance similarly, and claims that, "On the whole, the professional dance world is not one which promotes the emotional development to independence and individuality of its members" (1988b, p. 13). Dancers are trained to subordinate feelings and personal needs to the activity, and so, often do not develop the self-awareness which is necessary to emotional maturation. Social skills and development can be hindered by the isolation of technique classes. Dance teaching, Buckroyd says, has been greatly influenced by its history:

> Ballet developed in the hierarchical Old World in which concepts of inherent differences of value and importance between people (class differences and gender differences) were deeply embedded.
> The hierarchical and autocratic way of behaving has become deeply embedded in the culture of dance although the world around has changed a great deal. Even contemporary dance which was born into a very different social and political environment and taken up most enthusiastically by America where the culture is markedly more democratic, egalitarian and meritocratic, has inherited some of these old values. The legacy of this history is that the dance world, especially at a professional level, is hierarchical and oppressive. (1988b, p. 5)

As an example, she cites communications from teacher to student, choreographer to dancer, director to company which are insulting and abusive:

> I am talking about shouting, about name-calling, about sarcasm. I am talking about the failure to recognize dancers as responsible young people, about infantalising them and patronizing them. (1988b, p. 7)

In many companies, dancers are called "boys" and "girls" for the duration of their performing lives. The mode of interaction, Buckroyd says, is passed down with the technique: "It is all too easy to do as we have been done by" (1988b, p. 8). In order to help students grow as people as well as dancers, she suggests that in dance classes students need opportunities to take responsibility for their learning. They need practice in making choices and establishing preferences and priorities. They need the chance to make mistakes without the penalties being too severe. In short, they need the opportunities to experiment and explore within safe limits ... as the preliminary to taking charge of their own lives. (1988b, p. 14)

Additionally, to provide for the development of peer relationships, she says, "There should be some part of the class that calls for collaboration and cooperation between class members" (1988b, p. 15).

Buckroyd speaks out strongly against the idea that individual health or happiness be sacrificed to dancing. This, she says, amounts to

exploitation, seen most vividly in the tragedies of women such as ... Gelsey Kirkland. Balanchine cared for that mystical thing "dancing"; but he cared nothing for Gelsey Kirkland and she for a long time did not know how to care for herself. (1988b, p. 16)

The issues discussed on previous pages—the subordination of social and emotional developmental tasks to an emphasis of technical training and the emergence of quantitative thinking as an influence within the field—can be traced to a pervasive sense of dance as a competitive realm, a perception only encouraged by grant-making, by the imposition of business ethics on the arts, and by testing. The shift in values brought on by these trends serves to reinforce the hierarchical relations of the ballet world while discouraging the traditional modern dance values of freedom, risk-taking, and a subjective reinterpretation of form. What is seen and the way in which it is regarded have both been affected, making this shift in values among the most significant issues bearing on the character of today's modern dance.

Moreover, these are concerns which can be discussed in terms of gender. In modern America, dance classes are part of growing up for most middle-class girls and ballet, much more available than modern dance, is the prevalent influence. Many of those who go on to become professional are hooked at an early age, before they have developed any sense of self-awareness, and they grow up in dance, adopting the values of the field as their own. It is those values which teach that it is good to be obedient and·silent, good not to question authority or to have ideas which might conflict with what one is being asked to do. This kind of thinking produces followers, and is at odds with originality, critical thought, creativity, and artistry, effectively keeping many dancers out of leadership positions. Most male dancers begin training later in life, when verbal and social skills are more fully developed and they themselves are more rounded as people. Does the earlier onset of technical training for girls support the prevalence of men in leadership roles in dance today?[1]

Stress on following directions and focusing on the how rather than the why keeps dancers thinking technically and may explain, in part, why, as a field, dance now follows the market rather than taking the lead in determining its own direction. In *Women's Ways of Knowing* (1986), Mary Field Belenky and colleagues write of learning to find one's own voice. Learning to speak in a unique and authentic voice, they say, involves abandoning or going beyond the systems provided by authorities and creating one's own frame (p. 134). This is part of maturation, and this is what dancers must do to grow beyond technicians into artists. However, with the current stress on technical excellence throughout society as well as within dance, there is little support for going one's own way. Modern dance has only recently found acceptability and, at the moment, is loathe to risk losing it.

A number of issues which are central to this discussion, among them, the narrowness typical of dance training and the perception of a dance world with fixed values and standards into which one must fit, are raised by a 1988 study on meaning in dance. The teen-aged dance students interviewed in this study had no sense of dance as a human construction which they had the capacity to affect and change. They perceived their choices regarding dance as limited to whether or not

---

[1]Statistics on leadership are incomplete, but they seem to bear out the notion that men now dominate the professional dance field. Judith Lynn Hanna cites figures compiled in 1976, which assert that though 68% of the dance students and 55% of company members were female at that time, 73% of grant recipients were male. Of grantees receiving $70,000 or more, 100% were male (Hanna, 1987b, p. 46). The *1985 Annual Report of the National Corporate Fund for Dance* lists seven dance companies that received benefits from its 1985 campaign. All were directed by men, including Alvin Ailey, Merce Cunningham, and Paul Taylor. Eleven companies are listed in 1988, three directed by women. Ten years of *DanceMagazine* awards, from 1978–1988, have been divided among 22 men and 17 women. Since 1975, three women have been awarded the annual Capezio Award and 16 men. In 1987, the dance artist awarded the National Medal of Arts was Alwin Nikolais, and in 1988, it was Alvin Ailey. The Samuel H. Scripps American Dance Festival Award has, between 1981 and 1991, been awarded to seven men and six women.

to continue. "What are the costs of this state of affairs?" the authors asked.

> Whatever the human costs, some may feel that they are an inevitable consequence of having great art. We also see that there are consequences as well for the art. What is lost when a great many bright, articulate young women decide that there is no place in dance for them, because they do not have the "right body," or do not otherwise meet the requirements for the art as it now exists? To what extent does this restrict the development of the art, by allowing entrance only to those who will maintain the art as it is?
>
> Another issue which may reflect the costs of the current system is the disproportionate representation of men in positions of leadership and power in dance. We wonder about the relationship between this disproportionality and the emphasis on passivity and obedience in dance training, and the earlier age at which girls begin dance.
>
> We also must question whether it is indeed natural and inevitable that the system operate in this way, in which human lives are seen primarily as means to make great art, and the art itself is diminished by the loss of so many who might well have important contributions to make. Is it inevitable that art determine artists, rather than artists determining art? (Stinson, Blumenfeld-Jones, & Van Dyke, 1988, p. 183)

If long-term, rigorous technical training is the only way to produce versatile and skilled dancers, should not classes, also, from the start, teach the development of minds and emotional beings along with bodies? Delaying technical training until after the age of ten, teaching nonjudgmentally while providing information on safety and style, and allowing time for students to work out movement problems individually and together during class are all ways in which this might begin. Making discussion of why things are done as they are a part of learning technique is another. Providing a context for what is being taught will give students a clearer picture of a world in which they can make choices, as will linking a particular technique to a belief system. Dancers can learn to separate the person from the function if they are encouraged to strengthen both aspects.

All students desire the skills required for moving with power and articulation. That sense of control may be what draws many young women to the field, giving them a realm where they feel a certain empowerment. But that need not be the end of it. How best to teach physical skills without also teaching dependency, creating followers, and giving freedom only within the restrictions of the studio or the confines of a role—these are central issues for dance, both as a profession and as an art.

As Buckroyd has pointed out, relationships in this field are rarely democratic. The usual social structure is built around an autocrat (teacher or choreographer) and a group of disciples. An artist, like Balanchine, has ideas and then works in his/her medium to realize them. Dancers are the tools of choreographers. Can or should this change? Do we penalize a painter for wanting to work according to her/his personal vision? Are the stakes different in dance, where a choreographer is working with people rather than paints? What, if any, is the relationship between dance training and democratic traditions?

Perhaps the larger question is how much the world requires dance to stay as it is. By broadening the education of dancers the field will be transformed in ways that cannot be predicted. Providing the knowledge necessary to making choices and the tools with which to make their voices heard will prepare students to take their place within greater society and to bring dance as a field into line with the democratic ideals which form the basis for our culture. Certainly dancers will be less pliant, more questioning of how they are used, and more conscious of their own power, as well as more aware of the context and history of their art. There is little momentum in this direction today, however, as dance students prepare to compete for a small number of paying jobs, all of which emphasize technical versatility and excellence as a basic qualification. It remains to be seen how dance educators will reconcile the demands of the profession with a growing recognition that if the education of dance artists is limited, so, too, will be their art.

Photo by Lois Greenfield

Stephanie Skura and Company—1990 in "The
Fantasy World of Bernard Herrmann"

Stephanie Skura of Stephanie Skura and Company—1990

Photo by Tom Brazil

V

Modern Dance in a Postmodern World

Dance artists today concentrate much of their energy on packaging and image in order to participate in the market culture, coming increasingly under the influence of postmodern thought. There was a time, in the late 1960s and early 1970s, when there was a power in dance: dance seemed important to the cultural changes happening all around and would have a voice in reconstructing the world. Now, though many of the same artists are still at work, the feeling has changed. Within twenty years, dance has become peripheral to the world at large and seems to have only a cash connection with the society in which it resides. The gains in philosophic and aesthetic stature made with Duncan, Graham, and Judson have largely been lost. Presently, artistic values are more akin to those of dance artists in the nineteenth century, when aesthetic choices were most often guided by what the traffic would bear.

Previous chapters have presented an analysis of the relationship between cultural forces in the United States and the gradual shifting of principles and goals within modern dance, in an attempt to explain this evolution. Briefly restated, the argument is as follows.

Overview

Chapter I describes the lives and work of seminal dance artists before 1965, to establish a point of view which seems to speak for the original impulses behind the form. Mention is made of the efforts of early choreographers to create a dance which was uniquely American, within which artists could address significant and timely issues. Early dance artists saw themselves as leaders, as educators, demonstrating, with each new dance, the possibilities of the form. Modern dance was, in a sense, a calling, an expression of values which said that life and art are related as process and experience, and must express each other.

The contradictions between society's values and the original philosophic tenets of modern dancers are discussed at the end of the first chapter. Finally, the concept of postmodernism is introduced to describe a mode of consciousness which pervades American culture at the end of the 1980s, involving us with commercial values, commodification, and the lack of a moral or political agenda.

Chapter II focuses on an independent government agency, the National Endowment for the Arts, and demonstrates the ways in which that agency has, through its policies and practices, drawn modern dance into compliance with the market culture. It is noted that NEA approval has become a badge of excellence in the field, giving the agency undue authority in determining both business success and aesthetic trends. In addition, the make-up of the peer panels which decide on federal grants has been questioned, asking how objective they can be when they are selected by the program chair on the basis of her/his concept of "excellence."

Chapter III presents interviews with four dance professionals, all of whom have been active throughout the lifetime of the National Endowment for the Arts. The tensions between the culture and the art are felt in the field and have elicited a variety of responses among practicing dance artists. Each interview represents an individual point of view in a common field of endeavor. Kathy Posin and Liz Keen have continued living in New York for the duration of their careers, pursuing the role of the professional New York artist each in her own way. Each tends to view her problems in achieving financial stability within the evolving field as a personal failure, a character flaw which has hindered success in the dance market. Spider Kedelsky, on the other hand, left New York early and achieved real financial success with Dance/LA in California. And Jeff James represents another professional alternative—her decision to continue dancing after leaving New York necessarily pushed her into a leadership position, giving her a role in creating and shaping a dance community in Cincinnati.

It is interesting to observe that, in this group of four, the two who best understood the system set in place by the NEA are now both working within that system. Kedelsky has been a panelist and consultant for the NEA and James is director of a member organization of the NPN and has served as a panelist for a number of state arts agencies.

In Chapter IV, issues of training and education are addressed. The NEA's promotion of touring during the 1970s created more jobs for dancers, and as a result, dance programs within colleges and universities expanded rapidly to meet the demand, as did those in private studios. In response to the developing market, technical training has been given new emphasis within dance curricula, and ballet training is now acknowledged to be helpful— even necessary— to becoming a modern dancer. Because choreographers now rely on touring for survival, few maintain schools and fewer still have developed their own approach to technique. This wide acceptance of ballet serves to diminish stylistic diversity between modern companies and may, in fact, contribute to the increasingly prevalent gypsy mentality mentioned by Keen in Chapter III.[1]

As the philosophical underpinnings of ballet have begun seeping into modern dance, there has been a gradual acceptance of predetermined norms for technique, rather than thinking of movement as an idiosyncratic skill which both determines and is determined by an approach to choreography. In this atmosphere, the long-held values of individuality, originality, and experimentation and the notion that dance must

---

[1]The demise of the company school undoubtedly has many causes. With access to funding, companies no longer require the income provided by a school. Additionally, funders have, on the whole, emphasized touring and the performance of dance without encouraging the existence of small schools offering distinctive points of view. High rents in New York, where most major companies still operate, have made adequate space a problem. The most recent development in private dance training is the large studio organization which holds to no particular philosophical approach and offers a wide variety of classes and teachers in hopes of attracting as many students as possible.

seek a relevance to its time and place are brought into question. If the present narrow course in dance education persists, modern dance may soon face the same, widely acknowledged aesthetic crisis which now confronts ballet: a lack of resonant, insightful choreography, resulting in a reliance on spectacle and formal tradition. Another worry is that the present concentration on physical skills effectively hinders the development of outside interests, creating, for many dancers, a life without meaningful alternatives and a traumatic period of transition at the end of a performing career.

Modern Dance as an Art in a Postmodern Age

The unasked question throughout these chapters concerns the purpose of art and how modern dance fulfills that role. If one believes that art reflects culture, then modern dance is doing well, reflecting the market culture values which have overtaken American society. However, if art also has a role in influencing culture, a responsibility to teach, and to point up new ways of viewing the world, the system seems to have broken down.

The radical potential of art has been widely held to lie in the alteration of form. Janet Wolff (1981) cites Theodor Adorno, Bertholt Brecht, and Herbert Marcuse as sharing the view that a change in the expected, traditional form of art denies the audience an opportunity to relax and consume, and instead requires active participation. This emphasis on experimentation and the pursuit of a personal vision is creator-oriented art, where artists put their own values before those of the audience. Traditional, popular culture, on the other hand, is generally comfortable and affirming to the viewer and therefore, lulling. Even when the content is disturbing, if the form is conventional, the art is pacifying and not encouraging of critical awareness.

Brecht made a number of plays which break down traditional barriers between audience and performer, destroying illusion and revealing, rather than representing, social and political conditions. His aim was to jar the audience and hold them in the real world in the present time, so that all concerned were compelled to deal with the issues presented.

Wolff cites the difference between the music of Arnold Schoenberg and Igor Stravinsky. Both were innovative, but Schoenberg, with his twelve tone scale, changed music in a basic way, and so engaged the listener in an active, critical moment, while Stravinsky's music was only superficially new and so was still affirming.

The same distinction could be drawn between choreographers Merce Cunningham and George Balanchine. Balanchine worked in ballet, adding superficial modernisms such as flexed feet and off-center turns. Cunningham, on the other hand, has brought politics to the stage by doing away with traditional manipulation of the viewer's eye, declaring all dancers and all parts of the stage equal, and choreography independent of music. The audience is given new freedom as it must decide for itself where to look, whom to watch, and how to relate sound to vision.

From Isadora Duncan to Martha Graham to Yvonne Rainer, the energy behind modern dance has been the ongoing creation of new symbols which are strange and uncomfortably unfamiliar, in order to reveal the realities hidden behind accepted form. Now, as we enter the 1990s, is that role still available to dance artists? Technological advances have affected audience perception, reducing the difference between experiences. When distant cultures can be viewed on television or easily visited by airplane, the sense of wonder is diminished. American society has become less easily shocked and perhaps less willing to dig beneath the surface.

The 1980s have seen dance artists become consumer-oriented, trying to fit the values of the culture, to appeal to the audience and be accepted. Socialization has played a large role in this change, both the socialization of knowing that for certain kinds of work, funds are available, and that of realizing that, in today's market, with strong technical skills and a certain kind of body, it is possible to get a job as a dancer.

A Review of the NEA's Impact on Modern Dance

The Endowment states its mission as two-pronged: to foster excellence and diversity in the arts and to make the arts more broadly available. In promoting these goals, the NEA has reshaped the modern dance world from a disorganized group of small operations to a centrally focused national field of nonprofit, tax-exempt corporations with boards of directors. The availability of funding has had the effect of directing dance companies toward a business point of view. The NEA has further guided reorientation through the provision of funds for professional management, and by making evidence of management staff a credential of artistic professionalism for companies. The creation of arts management as a field in itself is one tangible result of NEA policies; it is the corporate world reproducing itself in the art world.

In accordance with the goal of making dance more widely available, a major aim at the Endowment has been to decentralize the modern dance field. To facilitate this, the NEA has provided funds to dance presenters nationwide, encouraging them to increase their presentations, bringing more dance to a wider audience. During the 1970s, many companies spent a good part of the year on tour. The Endowment has succeeded in developing a national market for modern dance companies, effectively expanding the field beyond New York City and providing both companies and dancers with work.

A troubling aspect to this activity lies in the decision-making process regarding who receives subsidy and promotion. In the late 1960s, the NEA began the Dance Touring Program with a short list of companies which met certain quality standards. Because touring was being so heavily promoted, decisions about which companies would be included on this list had a strong impact on the field, eventually dividing it between the approved companies and the unapproved. This imposed division necessarily had a major effect on hiring capabilities and organizational strength, as well as on the general perception of excellence. After some years, the Endowment made a switch to quantitative guidelines, saying, in effect, that professionalism could now be regarded as a question of numbers. At this point, the list expanded as companies were able to bring their operations into alignment with NEA stipulations. Finally, before phasing out the DTP altogether in 1984, the Endowment returned to qualitative guidelines, becoming more selective once again, and knocking long-time participating companies off the list.

The NEA cannot escape giving its imprimatur to those groups it supports. Perhaps this is most evident in the effect it has in guiding corporate and business giving. Many Endowment grants require the grantee to solicit matching funds (a 1:1 ratio) from private organizations before the money will be released. Some grants dictate an even higher ratio of private to federal money (3:1 or 4:1). Through this process, private foundations and corporations are encouraged to support those groups which meet Endowment standards. The NEA is, in effect, granting not only money but legitimacy and visibility as well, pointing out those groups deemed worthy. Some writers, among them Dick Netzer, Michael S. Joyce, and Samuel Lipman, have expressed worry that without NEA approval, a group cannot hope to attract private funding. Additionally, it has been noted that grant giving agencies increasingly consider business stability and growth as credentials in the arts, further ruling out those groups which choose to be marginal and/or community oriented in their work.

Netzer raises questions about the peer panel process which the NEA uses to decide which individuals and groups it will support. All panelists are chosen by the dance program director and staff, and are either former grantees or experts recognized and approved by the agency. This amounts to a closed loop: artists with dissenting points of view have little opportunity to be heard on a panel until they meet Endowment approval, which is not likely as long as they have dissenting points of view. Even without the list of the DTP, the NEA divides the dance world into the ins and the outs, simply on the basis of whether one is acceptable or not. Moreover, panels tend to reinforce their own biases and areas of acquaintance; there is a strong relationship between serving on a panel and receipt of NEA funding.

The make-up of panels is open to question as well. The agency states that an attempt is made to balance panels: the number of dance artists on any given panel rarely amounts to 50%, with the rest being taken up by administrators, presenters, dance writers, educators, and patrons. In effect, then, decisions on who receives Endowment support—the decisions which influence success with other funders and with presenters and which legitimate artists within their own field—are not being made by those actively involved in making art. By creating an administrative class which controls the dance market and then inviting these very managers and producers onto the panels which control funding, the Endowment has given a small group a very potent role to play in determining success within the field. Artistic leadership has been replaced by management.

Another aspect to the dilution of artistic leadership can be seen in the division of power within the corporate structure which governs dance companies today; nonartists on company boards share decision-making power with artistic directors. Paul Taylor's experience, described in Chapter II, would indicate that in today's dance world, a powerful board of directors is a necessity for financial well-being. Yet as the strength of these boards grows, their governing influence is bound to affect the quality and nature of the work produced (*Five Year Planning Document 1990–1994*, p. 5).

A question which arises frequently in literature about the Endowment concerns the benefits from NEA tax payer money. Is the NEA an agency for the support of artists and their work, or should the money it distributes benefit society more directly? If the latter, how does one best do that? By promoting art which pleases the general public? Or educates? Or decorates? Or perhaps by attempting to redress economic imbalances through training programs or by bringing regional distribution and racial factors to bear on funding decisions? Do established arts institutions have a legitimate right to continued support? Is it more important to provide funding for preservation or innovation? What are the priorities?

These are questions which the NEA has actively considered many times over, with each incoming administration and every defense of its budget, but the impact of these issues on aesthetic quality does not receive the same public attention. Moreover, the NEA does not acknowledge its influence in some areas. One such is the censorship implicit in funding guidelines and the manner in which these have shaped aesthetic activity during the past twenty years. In its Statement of Mission, the Endowment counsels itself not to "impose a single aesthetic standard or attempt to direct artistic content" (*NEA Annual Report 1987*, p. 222). Writer Steven C. Dubin (1987), however, suggests that funding is inherently a socialization process which validates some ideas and ignores others, inevitably causing artists to think in terms of what will be accepted and so, dictating the course of the field. In this way, all philanthropies become policy making institutions by definition.

There is another aspect to the relationship between aesthetics and funding, and here, the beginning of a pattern is revealed. When work is new and experimental and support is scarce, as in the 1930s and again in the 1960s, the aesthetic pares down to essentials, choosing function over decoration. With public acceptance and the availability of funds, the art adorns itself, allowing theatrical values more importance. We can see that in companies which have received steady support. There seems to be no correlation between adequate funding and innovation.

On the contrary, money tends to whet the appetite for more and bigger rather than for change. With this in mind, the question becomes, will the availability of continued support alter the tradition of reconception which has historically characterized modern dance? If current funding trends continue, a two-tiered dance field will develop—those with powerful organizations and strong funding histories and those without. Perhaps those outside the funding pattern, forced to live and work more marginally will, instead of feeling failure, begin anew to evolve a counter-cultural stance.

In its *Five Year Planning Document 1990–1994* (p. 5), the Endowment itself addresses this issue, wondering whether financial stability within the dance community is being achieved at the expense of quality or daring, whether the push to expand the audience has required a blanding, a dilution of the form, to make it more generally palatable. Though the NEA offers no further discussion, the very fact that the question has arisen indicates an answer. Once general accessibility becomes a goal in concert dance, marginal work with distinctive character is edged out. Dances must be designed for a wide variety of tastes.

Even in modern dance, technical brilliance has become increasingly important, replacing choreographic interest as the key element in the formula for success. Inevitably, as dance has been seen more widely, the response of lay audiences has become a significant issue, particularly as companies are encouraged to list the size of their audiences on grant applications. If dances and dance companies become commodities, packaged and marketed to attract buyers, then there must be quality standards upon which the average consumer can rely. Choreographic interest and innovation are difficult to gauge, especially for the unsophisticated eye. Technique, on the other hand, is easily recognizable, exciting, beautiful, and it separates "real" dancers from the rest of the world. In this way, the priorities of modern dance are shifting, turning to a more balletic point of view, and this has a strong influence on the way its students are taught.

The Endowment's Role: Dance as Commodity

Edward B. Keller (1984) describes the relationship between changing societal values and shifting funding patterns in the following way:

> An important element of the values revolution of the 1960s and 1970s, stemming from the psychology of affluence, was the rise of an egalitarian ethos, rooted in the conviction that in an era of unbounded economic vitality, economic and social well-being should be accessible to all segments of society. ... Now, with the recognition of new economic realities in the 1980s, egalitarianism is giving way to an emerging meritocracy orientation, a values perspective that ... allows those who have earned, or feel they have earned, a certain

status and position to actively seek mechanisms that distinguish themselves from others.

The arts explosion of the 1960s and 1970s . . . was fostered by the spirit of egalitarianism and pluralism, in which there was a desire to broaden exposure to and involvement in the arts.

The new meritocracy orientation will probably broaden the gap between the largest and most renowned arts organizations, which . . . are managing, and less well-established groups, many of which are threatened with bankruptcy. (p. 42–43)

This helps to explain the sense of crisis now being felt in some areas of the dance field. The market is contracting and competition is growing. When, in the 1970s, the NEA allocated significant funds to promote touring, a boom was created. Many companies were able to expand. Budgets increased as dancers were paid more equitably and managers were hired. Costumes, sets, and music became more important to the work. In order to continue on this scale in the years since the end of the Dance Touring Program, companies have directed their efforts to booking tours on their own, even as the decrease in funding has lessened the demand, and marketing has become increasingly important.

Within New York, certain venues, such as the Next Wave Festival at the Brooklyn Academy of Music or a Dance Theater Workshop production, have become highly sought after for the legitimation and validation they lend to a choreographer's work and for what they say about the level of acceptance he or she has achieved to date. The New York distribution system for modern dance has become part of the symbolic structure of career success within the field. The producers, BAM or DTW, however, have their own agendas, and in looking after their own images, tend to seek out artists who fit into the current trends. Tony Whitfield, associate director of the Lower Manhattan Cultural Council, sat on the 1988 Meta-Marketing Panel, mentioned in Chapter II, and had this to say about the measurement of careers within the dance world:

There is an unstated . . . graph of what a career is supposed to do, you know? It sort of goes along, at a certain point it goes up and up and up. . . . And it's marked by Next Wave [at BAM] if you're lucky enough to be there, and it's marked by the Joyce [Theater], and it's marked by being hot in Europe. And then it's marked by a drop. You know? And it's happening to people at very young ages . . . who are still vital.

And nothing's going on with the work, in fact the work is maturing, but the market. . . .

Whitfield paused and Elizabeth Zimmer, dance writer and moderator of the panel, finished his thought: "Your fifteen minutes has been spent." The panel agreed.

One concern with marketing in the arts stems from worry that young artists will become so inured to buying and selling that they will be unable to perceive the ways in which they, as artists, are affected. Perhaps this is happening already. Ann Cooper Albright, an organizer of the same Meta-Marketing Panel, spoke from the audience, saying that, in her view, the high-powered marketing which BAM does for the Next Wave Festival affects the general perception of careers in dance by creating a "criteria of success." In other words, the presence of that kind of marketing for some artists affects the way all artists are viewed. Even when artists choose to remain marginal, she said, performing in alternative spaces and not seeking a mainstream audience, without high-powered marketing, "it starts to look like not-success." This raises a number of possible futures. Will concern over image pressure dance artists to employ meta-marketing techniques simply to avoid the appearance of failure? Or will the limits of "success" be questioned, raising awareness of the definition currently driving the field?

The Endowment has long stressed making modern dance financially viable, which must, in the long run, mean adapting to the market, and inevitably, cause a dilution of purpose as a counter-cultural force. Whether an artist follows the guidelines in applying for grants or aims to sell art to producers and audiences, critical sensibility is dulled through participation. Choreographer Bill T. Jones, in discussing the changing role of artists, says:

> We live in a society that co-opts and absorbs everything . . . even the most avant garde work could be put on Johnny Carson . . . and millions would see it immediately and think it was groovy because it was so weird. . . . We don't have the moral authority any more. We're plugged into the same society. (Meta-Marketing Panel, 1988)

In a similar vein, C.S. Bromberg writes that in the 1980s, even experimental dance

> is not only expected to be intellectually stimulating; choreographers no less than audiences, now expect it to be

entertainment as well. The tradition of avant-garde experimentation which values the medium of dance for its own sake, embracing complexity and seeking to explore the fundamental propositions of what its art consists in during its own time, now slumber under the choreographer's concern for the audience and his or her career. Those few who challenge the established logic ... are branded as irresponsible or self-indulgent. Often, this criticism is justified: it is difficult to respect radical conclusions when they are presented from within the very systems of ideas and institutions they supposedly seek to undermine. In a society where all art, no matter how daring or reckless, is bought, there can be no avant-garde. (1981, p. 9)

The daily experience of choreographers seeking funding reinforces the necessity of participating in the culture according to predetermined standards, whether they be company balance sheets showing a certain amount of growth, a board of directors reflecting a racial and cultural mix, adequate audience interest in company concerts, or a performance schedule with a sufficient number of shows listed. This, as was noted in Chapter I, is a result of what Fredric Jameson has described as the all-enveloping market culture, a historical shift which must be acknowledged to understand developments in art of the late twentieth century.

Along with stressing the financial viability of dance, in its self-appointed role as caretaker for the arts, the NEA has inevitably centralized power and authority within the field. In spite of the agency's efforts at being responsive, a single, Endowment-influenced vision of what dance is has slowly begun to prevail. Tony Whitfield comments on the power of the NEA point of view:

I think there's a larger vision of what American dance and performance art and culture is supposed to be about. And it's largely— it happens in panels at the National Endowment. It happens in panels in the organizations that are supported by the National Endowment. ... I think there's an issue of, like, this is American culture. This is what we're going to market. This is where it's going to go. ... There is a hierarchy [in New York] ... it is BAM, DTW, PS 122, and maybe, every once in a while it sort of shifts around, but that's where it is, if you look at the press. ... (Meta-Marketing Panel, 1988)

The implication is that the distribution system, the press, and the Endowment serve to reinforce each other, restricting the definition of what is acceptable. This idea is supported by the fact that dance writers and presenters make up a significant portion of NEA panels. The resulting vision, Whitfield says, is limited and largely excludes Third World artists and those working outside the accepted stream: "It really is an issue of whether you fit into the American vision of what the arts are, because ... there is no money to continue careers that do not fall into that pattern." This is my reading of the situation too, and seems to explain the funding and work problems which have plagued Posin and, in a less severe way, Keen. When a choreographer's work goes out of style, he or she is discontinued, which, in a centralized system, amounts to suppression.

Careerism among Dancers

Both Posin and Keen mention that as choreographers, they were at the mercy of their dancers, so to speak—that at certain points they were working with people who knew their repertory but who were not completely in tune with their goals and ideas. And as Keen says, it is particularly important for modern dance choreographers to work with dancers who are in philosophic and aesthetic agreement because of the individual nature of the work.

The problem is one which came into being as companies acquired funds to offer salaries—a development welcomed by most dance artists—and dancing began to become a job. Many dancers have become mercenaries seeking out opportunities to be seen onstage and to make money, hoping to build their careers. Since few choreographers today have schools, hiring is often done by audition, linking choreographers with dancers they may never have met before. Many dancers will dance with whomever will hire them, without commitment to a particular artist or style or philosophical impulse. If a choreographer is touring heavily and/or receiving press attention, he or she is especially desirable because there will be more work and a better known name to list on a resume.

This is close to the work ethic of many corporate employees. According to sociologist Ann Swidler (1980), those who do best in corporate life are often those who lack any sort of guiding philosophy which might cut them out of one market or another. They are the ones always ready to go. Settling down implies a dead end. Increasingly, this might apply to both choreographers and dancers. Careers with the greatest prestige demand readiness to travel, going from one organization to another, from one role to another. The emphasis is on keeping the options open, which means an avoidance of commitment, in order to develop the self, the career. Finding the "right place" (or company or teaching job) is a contradiction because it has become wrong in terms of how we conceive growth. The only right solution is to have a set of ideas and skills contained within the self which can be perpetually renewed, always shifting into original patterns. One's self is one's only resource. This loss of context, grounding, or community is demonstrated by a resistance to any kind of commitment and the sense of isolation shows up in art which depicts a reified society overwhelming the individual, such as, in literature, *Slaughterhouse Five* and *One Flew Over the Cuckoo's Nest*.

A Loss of Purpose: Education's Role

In dance, the loss of context is not only visible in the art but felt in the lack of community within dance companies. As dance artists have involved themselves in the market culture, the loyalty and sense of purpose described by the early moderns have disintegrated. Careerist tendencies on the part of both choreographers and dancers have reduced the working relationship to that of employer/employee. Roles have, in a sense, shifted. Many dancers no longer expect to sacrifice throughout their careers, waiting on tables in order to work with a chosen company. Though they may still be poor, the expectation now is that jobs are available.

For choreographers, it is assumed that as they move up the ladder, they will be able to pay for dancers as well as for costumes, music, and lighting. Success today requires maintaining a business which involves publicity, bookkeeping, regular rehearsal space, and nonprofit, tax-exempt status. This kind of operation is hard-won and serves to separate mature choreographers from younger dancers, emphasizing hierarchy within the field and isolating successful artists in defensive, conservative positions.

The major threats of the market culture to the arts seem to lie in the competition for attention, grant money, jobs, and roles, coupled with the change in social relations and the shift in values illustrated by the widespread belief among choreographers that as one progresses, one must make use of increasing amounts of money in order to project the image of success. These are the changes felt in the daily lives of dance artists which influence the aesthetic choices made, and this is where education is needed: to raise awareness of the forces now at work shaping the culture and so increase the possibilities for artistic response.

Instead, however, dance programs in colleges and universities have, for the most part, fallen in with the shift in values and have begun emphasizing technical and performance skills. They are responding both to the general trend within higher education to promote professional goals and training and to the demand from the field for more and better dancers. Moreover, they have institutionalized their aims in an accreditation agency, the National Association of Schools of Dance, for the purpose of demonstrating to administrators, potential students, and the lay public that standards are being maintained and that, on the whole, schools are doing a good job of training future dance professionals.

For many years, the demanding technical training necessary to a professional dance career was a reason for the uneasy accommodation of dance within the university. Technical training was opposed to the broad based, generally accepted concept that education was for the whole person. However, as discussed in Chapter IV, university programs have made an effort to gain credibility within the professional field, and often, the best of what a university education had come to mean has been lost in the attempt.

Several years ago, John Gamble, head of the Dance Department at UNC-Greensboro, devised two lists to describe his idea of what a university dance program should be offering the dance student. Under "university," he wrote the words knowledge, integration, personal development, the ability to make choices, permission to be critical, and learning from the inside out. Under "private training" came skill, craft (through a style), demands of the discipline, training students to fit into a mold, acceptance of what is given, and learning from the outside in. These lists make a clear distinction between education and training and point up what is lost when concentration is on the latter. As it is, most dancers learn to think technically, narrowing their concerns to rehearsing, physical mastery, and survival issues: how to get work, how to write grants, how to cope with injuries, who is doing what. Dance students are trained not to question except as to how and what; there is little encouragement for asking why. Is it any wonder that the dance of the 1980s has been essentially concerned with itself?

The narrowness of training also impacts on the political aspect of dancers' lives, denying them knowledge of the machinery which runs the society in which they function. Without exposure and encouragement, participation in the outside world will necessarily be limited. Nowhere in training do dancers learn to address society, to question or determine their own role in the culture. Doubtless, the discipline, with its emphasis on silence, received knowledge, and imitation, adds to the problem. Is there a relationship between daily training in accepting direction and the fact that business values have been allowed to shape the profession with little influence exerted in return? Careers are buffeted by social forces which artists would rather not engage, and most have been only too happy to turn over the administrative chores to others, allowing management to fall to people versed in the ethics of business. In so doing, the field has let go the reins of both the profession and the art. As the culture has evolved, dance artists have not learned to take care of their own affairs.

Without an understanding of cultural forces and the historical role of the arts, how can any art hope to survive on its own terms? How will the artistic viewpoint find acceptance if it cannot be voiced effectively? When education isolates, the means of control has been lost. In the *American Dance Guild Newsletter*, Angela Allyn writes about the paradox of dancer/choreographers

> seeking increased levels of funding from corporations, foundations, and government ... [when] they feel somehow apart or exempt from some of the realities of the entities they turn to for support. For instance, they don't lobby for tax revisions that influence exemptions encouraging corporate gifts. Or they are vaguely aware of the products that these corporations ... produce. How many choreographers read the business page of the newspaper ... ? How many dancers understand or even care about the nature of the formation of foundations? ... How many ... get out and campaign for candidates who will support the arts? ... The arts are an integral part of society only if the artists help it to be so. The artist determines whether his work is the passive mirror or the active hammer of society. (1987, p. 8)

The fluctuation and fickleness of the market is a relatively new phenomenon in dance, creating overnight sensations—the flavor of the month—and then moving on. Star consciousness, an emphasis on technique, and a de-emphasis on education combine in this economy to create problems for the older dance artist—both for the choreographer whose work is no longer in vogue and for the dancer no longer able to sustain a performing career. Arlene Croce, dance critic for the *New*

Yorker, makes mention of this in a long article about former Balanchine dancer Edward Villella, now director of the Miami City Ballet. She writes:

> Villella is the only ballet star I've ever heard of who has been through four years of college. [At family insistence, he attended the New York Maritime College and earned a BS degree in marine transportation.] The experience ... is one that he is grateful for; it put him in a class apart from other dancers, able to fend for himself and choose what he would be. (1988, p. 53)

That power to "choose what he would be" is what dancers lack when they have only one skill and only one way of approaching the world. When the years of performing are over, with no interests outside the studio, there are few options for a satisfying and fulfilling second career.

Concern about the early and inevitable transition which dancers must make has begun to surface. In its *Five-Year Planning Document 1990– 1994*, the National Endowment for the Arts notes a growing awareness of the problem and characterizes its response as "part of the Dance Program's exploration of professional training in the field" (p. 26). This seems an appropriate place to look; likely, the long, narrow path the dance student walks sets the limits of his or her life, goals, interest, and vision. When one's teachers and models give no import to experience outside the dance studio or to a contextual understanding of one's art, it is easy to dismiss these as unnecessary, both to life and to dancing.

A Personal Response

The National Endowment for the Arts has shaped the world of modern dance in two major ways. Through its funding policies it has influenced dance companies and careers, and in this way, has had an effect on the kind of dances being produced. And, less directly, due to its influence on the aesthetics of the field, Endowment policy has begun to shape the way young dancers are educated, going so far as to suggest standardized testing in the arts.

In terms of education, the arguments above have persuaded me that without a change in the priorities for dance students, dancers will continue internalizing the very values which most threaten the ability to develop a voice as artists and citizens. Many creative artists are reclusive by nature, like Posin, preferring to "spend the time in the studio and let the fundraising go." But it is more than fundraising which is at stake. Isolation in the studio will not effect change. I would like to believe that early exposure to the ideas which impel our culture will lay the ground for later involvement, by providing knowledge and basic understanding. Taking part requires comprehending reality in order to discover ways of making decisions for the self and for the field within that context. We must give ourselves time for education.

The effect of dance training on personality, goals, and life pattern is a fairly urgent question, since, as a discipline, we persist in starting training for young girls at an early age. Are we intensifying the already present perception of dance as women's work? What are the long-term implications for modern dance as an art if we continue in this direction? Should choreography students be given a different educational background from dancers? Might there be a negative correlation between leadership ability and dance training?

We want to develop dance skills, yes, and also language skills, decision-making skills, and social skills, along with an understanding of the world. If one accepts John Gamble's description of the key to creative artistry as "the power to have opinions," then it is no good training dance students to obey without question, to fit a form, or accept imposed standards. Though I understand the thinking behind it, by the same token, the NEA's plan for devising tests in the arts is filled with risk, raising the possibility of national norms of good and bad, and effectively denying the power of subjective response. It is a policy which cannot help but extend the influence of the Endowment on the production of art in this country, guiding audience as well as artist to pre-approved choices.

In the professional realm, Endowment influence has been profound and not without controversy. The issue of judging work and careers is a tricky one. When, in the late 1960s, with the intent of making the Dance Touring Program as strong as possible, the NEA began imposing restrictive, qualitative standards for eligible companies, they opened themselves up to criticism about imposing a style and taste on the country as a whole. In the mid-1970s, the DTP adopted quantitative standards, and at the time, I thought it was a positive move. The change gave companies like mine, existing outside the New York, postmodern dance world, a chance to conform numerically to NEA guidelines and join the prestigious list. The range of groups who were able to qualify by this means was great, however, evoking an outcry about the dilution of standards and the inappropriateness of using quantitative measures to determine artistic substance. The Endowment eventually changed back to qualitative guidelines throughout all programs.

Later, when, in the last years of his tenure, then-Chairman Hodsoll began pressing for a return to the more objective, quantitative measure, Endowment staff and directors resisted. Hodsoll was proposing that grant amounts be determined by

> ... relating an institution's artistic ranking to its budget size.
> . . .
> The change in the outcome of this new ... process would be great: if budgets were to be a required factor in determining amounts, larger-budget applicants, in a time of flat Endowment appropriations, would receive increased funding, while smaller-budget applicants would receive less. The signal sent to the world of art would be clear: henceforth, artistic achievement would properly be judged by money, not art. (Lipman, 1989, p. 7)

Such a change would have cut back on staff and directorial power and involved a major change in the functioning of the peer panels. In the long run, however, the equation of size with excellence has not been seen as helpful in the arts, although clearly, it is happening anyway. The vast open market within which we now work strongly influences both those who present dance and those who make it to think in economic terms. The market promotes an awareness of what will sell and so skews expectations of what is "best," as well as the perception of success itself. By rewarding fiscal accomplishment and audience appeal, the funding system underlines those values.

How can a numerical system work fairly without negating the impulse for innovation and experimentation? Perhaps policy could be adapted to the idea that smallness and regionalism encourage diversity by setting up varying, non-hierarchical categories to accommodate and encourage differing aspirations within the field. The choice not to seek a broad market will have to be recognized and rewarded in order to foster character and point of view, aspects which often make art controversial.

The one area where I think the NEA has genuinely sought individuality and uniqueness is in the Choreographer's Fellowships. With the development of the National Performance Network and the stipulation that participating presenters produce work by at least two Choreographic Fellowship winners each season, will we now see the growth of competition at this level with a market awareness developing here too? How can it best be made clear that bigger is not necessarily better and that growth is not required for continued support?

John K. Urice has suggested that the NEA restrict itself to making large block grants to national treasure institutions (to be defined by the National Council on the Arts) and award more and larger grants to the states for the direct support of small organizations and individual artists (1991, p. 8). This would take the Endowment out of the role of "king-maker" and give responsibility for funding the less well-known to local councils. Such a system might well slow the imposition of a national standard and encourage the development of diversity in the arts based on place and local culture.

Clearly we need more understanding of the effect of funding policies both on modern dance as an art and on the lives of dance artists before we can point the way with any degree of certainty. At the moment, the Endowment, in its ongoing effort to broaden the audience base, is turning to video and television as a means of distribution, and the market will soon be affected in another, as yet unknown manner. The choices made here, as to who is funded and which groups are featured, will influence assumptions and beliefs about dance for many years to come. A realistic understanding of effect would be very helpful in deciding what is desirable and what can be achieved.

In terms of the Endowment's role in the lives and work of dance artists, the NEA must, I think, begin public discussion of shifts in policy, to allow response from the field. At present, an effort is made to hold open meetings throughout the country every so often, allowing artists access to agency officials. In addition, in 1990, the NEA Dance Program conducted a survey of choreographers in four major metropolitan areas, trying to assess economic conditions within the field. As far as I know, however, the broad field of artists is not given an opportunity to comment on proposed funding policy before it goes into effect.

To my mind, the circle of influence must be widened; for many years too much authority has been given to too few. This would include opening the makeup of peer panels to question. Under the present system, critics and administrators serve on panels in equal numbers to artists. Writing in the *Movement Research Journal*, Sarah Shulman says she thinks panels should be 100% artists. "As it stands today," she writes,

> the person who has the power to allow or deny you a booking or give you a good or bad review is the same person who is going to decide whether or not you receive a grant and the

same person who gives out awards at the end of the season. Such a system is ripe for corruption and should be discontinued. (1991, p. 3)

Should not a high percentage of those making funding decisions in the arts be artists? And should they not forfeit the right to apply to their own panel for that cycle? Or perhaps to any panel? Maybe for artists, serving on a panel should be construed as a call to service, a draft of sorts. At the least, the system for selecting artist-panelists must be rethought. Excellence is a subjective point of view, and when the selection of panel participants rests on such a criterion, in essence, inclusion becomes a matter of personal choice, resting on the subjective approval of the Dance Program director and staff. This means that artists whose work is controversial in NEA terms, or divergent in some way, have little chance of representation. It also means that most panelists are probably chosen because they or their work are already known to those choosing, serving to heighten the impression that the NEA funding process is a closed circle.

A more representative, democratic means of selection might involve a registry of artists based on Posin's suggested criteria: integrity, longevity, and demonstrated activity within the field. It has even been suggested that, given a registry of this sort, a lottery might be the fairest way to select panels and/or distribute funds, ridding the process of personal taste, political considerations, and networks. The outcry one could expect at a development of this sort would probably signify that politics and taste are arbiters which we are not willing to do without. Perhaps a rotating list of all applicants for NEA funding would provide a more representative selection. If such a list revolved regularly, far fewer artists would be excluded from the decision-making process, helping to make the NEA a force in which the artistic field plays a significant role, and removing grounds for the suspicion that a point of view has been set in place by the very process of selecting panels.

No doubt, with a larger pool of available panelists, Endowment funding priorities would be far less settled. There would be less agreement in general, and there would certainly be protestations from those who hold to immutable standards. However, if, as a country, we seek, with public money, to allow a series of limited, pre-approved panels to decide whose art will be set apart by the NEA imprimatur, we are denying the tradition of democracy which makes us uniquely free as a people. In my view, the diversity of our culture is, especially in the arts, a sign of health. If allowed to flourish, artistic plurality will lead us to—will in fact demand—dialogue, keeping all those involved in the arts actively questioning, and I would hope, allowing a resurgence of resonant leadership on the part of artists.

The concerns mentioned here will no doubt raise responses from many readers involved in the dance world. It is important that dance artists begin speaking out, giving voice to their perspective. The field is changing, and along with it, the experience of dancing. If we do not speak out and participate in these changes, working to make them more humane and reflective of our belief systems, we will lose the chance to take part in shaping the values of our field. As long as we rely on critics and managers to do the speaking for us, we must accede to their interpretation of both our art and our lives, and in the long run, to their interpretation of our role as artists, as well.

AFTERWARD:
April 10, 1991

A Crisis in the Arts

It has been two years since the body of this manuscript was completed. During that time, a critical debate over arts funding has come to the fore throughout the country, raising questions about censorship, obscenity, and the very definition of art itself. At this writing, the United States is in recession. State budgets are being trimmed and arts organizations throughout the country wait and wonder how they will survive the next round of cuts.

The combination of fiscal retrenchment with a resurgence of national mistrust for the art world has deeply hurt the cause of government arts funding, and as a result, the arts face new restraints on many levels. For example, Jefferson James (1991) reports that Governor Voinovich of Ohio has proposed a 60% cut in the state arts budget. If successful, this move will decimate what has, up to now, been the third largest state arts budget in the United States. In New York, historically the largest state arts budget in the United States, Liz Keen says that the "budget is poised to be cut by 50%. If the cuts are not that drastic, they still will be significant" (1991). Nationally, the Bush Administration has proposed a 1992 budget which increases funds for all federally connected arts institutions (such as the Smithsonian Institution and the National Gallery of Art), but keeps the National Endowment for the Arts budget flat at $174 million. In addition, the federal proposal hikes the National Endowment for the Humanities allocation to $178 million, surpassing that of the NEA for the first time since their joint founding in 1965 (Kastor, 1991, p. C1). And on the level of local funding, Guilford County in North Carolina has decided, as of March 20, 1991, to withdraw all support for the arts (*Greensboro News & Record*, March 24, 1991, p. B2).

Political ambivalence is clearly set out in fiscal language here. The significance of these actions transcends budgetary considerations. While the loss of support is painful, requiring serious reconsideration of priorities and goals on the part of arts organizations, these moves are perhaps most harmful in the long run because of the signals they send. To withdraw government arts funding is to withhold public affirmation of art as an important and fundamental part of community life.

Lourdes Lee Valeriano, writing in the *Wall Street Journal* (March 22, 1991, p. B10B), chronicled the financial desperation in the dance world under the headline "Pennsylvania Ballet, Other Companies Face Swan Song if Funds Don't Rise." Valeriano writes that the recession has sharply reduced financial support to the arts from both government and private sources while competition for funding has increased. This has particularly hurt dance companies because they are labor intensive organizations dependent on donations for up to 50% of their income.

In the article, Bonnie Brooks, executive director of Dance U.S.A., an association of eighty professional dance companies, describes the situation as one of paring budgets, laying off dancers, and cutting back the number of programs and performances. Companies are "creating short-term emergency plans to stay operational," according to Brooks. David Oakland, general manager of the Cleveland/San Jose Ballet, is quoted as saying that we are experiencing "the beginning of a transition for all major dance institutions for this country. . . . Organizations are going to pull in and tread water." Valeriano goes on to suggest that dance appears to be losing funds to social concerns such as the environment and health care, priorities which even arts afficianados find it difficult to counter. As manager Oakland himself notes, "It's hard to argue for dollars for performing arts when there are people who are homeless."

Whatever the balance of the 1990s holds, assumptions about the place of art in American society have come under question. Moreover, the harsh economic realities brought on largely by the fiscal policies of the Reagan/Bush era are challenging our suppositions about the influence and endurance of American arts institutions (FEDAPT, 1991, p.7). Though concern in the art world has largely been focused on the National Endowment for the Arts, a symbol of stability and continued government support in a time of crisis, the situation is more complex than the question of whether or not federal funding is continued.

FEDAPT, an organization which provides assistance to performing artists and performing arts institutions, has given over part of its *1989–1990 Annual Report* to drawing a concise picture of the financial circumstances facing the art world today. The report notes that the past ten to fifteen years have seen a convergence of factors which has sharply altered the environment in which artists and arts groups function. It then goes on to explain that "This crisis is not about incompetent management or bad managers. It is not about lack of accountability or bad boards. It is not about unappreciated productions or bad art, either" (FEDAPT, p. 11). FEDAPT characterizes the situation as a crisis brought about largely by three factors: (1) financial shifts and the debt culture, (2) the shrinking human capital pool, and (3) overregulation and stagnation in the arts community itself. The situation is described in the following way:

(1) Since NEA support rarely represents more than a small percentage of contributed income, no individual or organization can point to cuts in NEA funding as a fatal blow to budgets or operations. The realignment of private sector funding sources, however, has become a serious problem. Reagan/Bush policies have withdrawn federal support from domestic human resource programs, creating a gap which non-federal funding sources have been pressed to fill, moving their focus away from the arts. Nonfederal funding had represented a significant percentage of contributed income to the arts, and the redirection of that resource has created serious stress. Moreover, financial strain has been increased by tendencies in the not-for-profit arts movement to view growth as the primary indicator of success. This perceived need to grow has encouraged many organizations to expand operations beyond their level of real income, thus accumulating debts which are

debilitating, if not life threatening. Most major dance companies find themselves in this position today (Valeriano, 1991).

(2) The development of the not-for-profit arts field in the 1970s coincided with the coming of age of the baby boom generation, providing a large pool of young, educated, and affluent urban dwellers, an ideal audience for the growing performing arts industry. Moreover, this group was entering the job market as many arts organizations were starting up, and a large number accepted the learn-as-you-go entry level jobs available in these organizations. Today, as this generation ages, members face increased demands on their time and finances as they raise children and move away from the inner city. They are a less available audience with less money to spend. Many of those employed in the arts have left for jobs which can support families, and those who have stayed have moved up into senior management positions. Meanwhile, the traditional model for arts organizations, designed in the 1960s and 1970s, continues to rely heavily on human capital for middle management functions such as fundraising and development. Arts organizations with these structures now face a shortage of inexpensive, educated labor as well as a diminished audience.

(3) According to FEDAPT, the length of time and the degree to which an industry responds to public policy, regulations, and funding guidelines and accountability, rather than the open marketplace, will determine the amount of overregulation. In the extreme, an industry can become so concerned organizationally, managerially, and strategically with responding to requirements laid out by the government that they lose the memory of how to function in an unregulated set of conditions. When faced with radical shifts in the environment, such as those now facing the arts community, the response from the industry is a cry for more government help, a clamoring for change in public policy to provide increased resources or more favorable operating conditions. The arts industry has, since 1965 and the founding of the NEA, become dependent on public policy, unable to function outside a regulated environment without massive reorganization.[1]

---

[1]On August 15, 1991, FEDAPT sent out a letter detailing its dissolution as a corporate entity. Explaining that today's realities require an approach for which FEDAPT was not equipped, Nello McDaniel, director of the organization wrote, "Given the rapid deterioration of conditions in the field during the last year, [associate director] George [Thorne] and I believe that more radical measures are called for. ... Our work in the future can't simply be about fixing broken

Response from the Press

In the past two years, the National Endowment for the Arts has undergone a struggle for survival, fighting charges from all sides. From the right have come assertions that too much government support has gone to art which the average American finds offensive, if not pornographic; from the art world have come allegations of betrayal as the NEA has fought to defend itself against charges of elitism and the support of obscenity. For some months, artists accepting federal grants were asked to pledge that government money would not be used to fund obscenity, "including, but not limited to, depictions of sadomasochism, homoeroticism, the exploitation of children, or individuals engaged in sex acts" (Henry, 1990, p. 85). Citing the threat to their right of free expression, some artists refused grants rather than sign, and a number of suits were filed by artists and arts organizations against the NEA. The pledge requirement was dropped in October 1990. Meanwhile, however, in the summer of 1990, the National Council on the Arts had denied four applications approved by peer panels, on the basis that the four performance artists involved were engaged in work with significant sexual content—a signal that confusion about policy and priorities has blurred the normally clear lines of leadership within the government industry.

The press has covered the situation closely, and for many months, the question of government support for the arts has been argued by pundits across the nation. The debate has been wide-ranging. Those supporting restrictions on federal funding for the arts have reasoned that taxpayers have the right to control what their tax dollars buy. Arguing against this line, Tom Wicker has reminded readers that other dissenting groups, such as war protesters, have never had such a right. He also brought up the question of whether or not denying funds to certain kinds of work amounts to censorship. In Wicker's opinion, which echoes the ideas of Michael Useem discussed in Chapter II, the probable result can be more precisely described as self-censorship:

> If no government support is permissable for some art and some artists, while other art and other artists are federally

---

arts organizations. ... We believe that our next phase of work might be best characterized ... as 'action research'—that is, rather than studying what has been, we must explore ways in which we can effectively intervene to influence and ignite arts evolution and change."

supported, the chilling effect would be powerful on those artists who might otherwise choose to work in the proscribed and ineligible forms. ... [this kind of selective funding] will tend to make all artists more cautious and less challenging in applying for grants—a chilling effect indeed. (1990, p. A15)

James J. Kilpatrick put forward the opinion that government has no business funding art in the first place. If, he wrote, a panel of poets at the NEA is charged with awarding fifty fellowships, the result is a subjective decision creating an arbitrary distinction:

In any such competition ... the difference between No. 50 and No. 51 is minute. Judgments are entirely subjective. It is all a matter of the panel's taste. But the upshot is that No. 50 gets $20,000 of the taxpayers' money, plus the fame and recognition that goes with being an NEA Fellow.

Well, you say, that is how the world is. Some win, some lose. This is true enough in the private sector, but it ought not to be true in the public sector. Our government has no business creating winners and losers with public money. In a free society, poets, painters and pianists ought to compete in a free marketplace. If their work catches on, fine. If not, this is how the world really is. (1990, p. E4)

Art critic Robert Hughes, writing in *Time Magazine*, quoted North Carolina senator Jesse Helms as being of the same mind. "I have fundamental questions," says Helms, "about why the Federal Government is supporting artists the taxpayers have refused to support in the marketplace" (1989, p. 82). Hughes took Helms to task for that remark, explaining that

this was exactly what the NEA was created, in 1965, to do— and it was the wisest of decisions. Lots of admirable art does badly at first; its rewards to the patron are not immediate and may never come. Hence the need for the NEA. It is there to help the self-realization of culture that is not immediately successful. (1989, p. 82)

Responding to arguments that support for the arts ought to be coming from the private sector, in the same article, Hughes defends the role of the federal government as grantmaker. Ironically, here one of the early criticisms of the government agency's power has become useful to Hughes as a defense. Corporations, he says, are not likely to have an easy time deciding to support demanding or controversial work. Corporate money "is nervous money," he writes. "It needs the NEA for reassurance as a Good Housekeeping Seal of Approval."

Some criticism of the Endowment has arisen from a distrust of the peer review panel process. James J. Kilpatrick spent time investigating that process and came up with results similar to those described in Chapter II for 1987. Kilpatrick researched the Endowment's *1989 Annual Report* for information on the dance panels. "Let us talk about grantors and grantees," he writes. "I find the relationship chummy." He goes on to describe the makeup of several panels and to list the grants awarded to those serving. For example, he lists the six members of the Challenge II panel and reports that five of those six were awarded funds:

> [Bonnie] Brooks won a $55,000 grant through a panel on interarts.
> [Laura] Dean won $100,000 from the panel on dance companies.
> [Myrna Saturn] Gatty's Southern Arts Federation won eight grants from various panels totaling $820,000.
> [Heinz] Poll won a $10,000 grant "to support the development of new work by Artistic Director Heinz Poll for the Ohio Ballet."
> [Gus] Solomon's company won a $19,000 grant "to support domestic touring, general management representatives, and the creation of collaborative work by Artistic Director Gus Solomon." (*Greensboro News & Record*, March 24, 1991, p. B4)

"You get the picture," Kilpatrick went on. "Artist A is on Panel B that awards a grant to Artist C who serves on Panel D. Artist E's panel awards a grant to Artist A. So it goes, so it goes, so it goes."

Bonnie Brooks quickly responded to this column in a letter to the *Washington Post*. Her letter affirmed that while she was a panelist the organization by whom she is employed received grants from the Endowment, but, she said,

> It is not true that there was any cause and effect between my services and the awarding of federal grant monies to my employers. In fact, the Endowment's conflict-of-interest rules prevent any panelist from reviewing applications with which they have any connection or vested interest. Charges of cronyism wrongly dismiss what I know to be serious and rigorous process. . . .
> Mr. Kilpatrick seems unaware that all advisory panel recommendations are reviewed by the National Council on the

Arts, a presidentially appointed body. . . . Final decisions regarding all grant awards are made by the chairman of the
Endowment for the Arts. These procedural layers ensure the
wise and appropriate expenditure of public funds. (April 8,
1991)

A major question emerging from the ongoing debate has concerned
exactly what art should be and the role it ought to play in American
society. Samuel Lipman, for example, publisher of the *New Criterion*
and a former member of the National Council on the Arts, was quoted
in a letter from Linda Winfield to the *Greensboro News & Record*. Winfield used Lipman's words to make the point that much work which is
currently controversial is questionable as art:

> The simple fact is that this cutting edge art . . . is concerned
> not with art but with advocacy, not with the creation of
> permanent beauty but with the imposition of hitherto re-
> jected modes of behavior and ways of living. (1990, p. A8)

These words give rise to questions regarding the purpose of art and
its place in American culture. Sculptor Frederick Hart, whose works
include the Viet Nam Memorial statue, has not been surprised to see
the NEA coming under fire. He wrote in the *Washington Post* that, in
his opinion, the art world of today plays the role of intellectual bully,
operating "on a belief system of deliberate contempt for the public. . . .
Once," he claimed, "under the banner of beauty and order, art was a
rich and meaningful embellishment of life, embracing—not desecrat-
ing—its ideals, its aspirations and its values" (1989, p. A19). Today, art
is involved with aggrandizing itself at the expense of sacred public
sentiments embodied by symbols such as the flag and the crucifix. This
stance, he says, has cost the art world any claim on moral authority.

> Look about you. The artlessness of contemporary life has
> come about because of a breakdown in the fundamental
> philosophy of art and who it is created for. The flaw is not
> with a public that refuses to nourish the arts. Rather it is
> with a practice of art that refuses to nourish the public. . . .
> Moral authority is the critical element by which a society
> regards art either as an essential and meaningful part of life,
> as in Renaissance Italy or, as today, a superfluous bit of
> fluff mainly indulged in by a small snobbish minority. (1989,
> p. A19)

Ellen Goodman has also decided that the art world has lost touch with mainstream America. On October 9, 1990, she wrote a column in the *Washington Post* warning artists that it is time to attend to the issues of "class, elitism, artistic sensibilities and common sense." In her eyes, the art world has brought trouble on itself. The funding woes of the NEA cannot be blamed on Jesse Helms and other rightists, she wrote, but

> are the fault . . . of an art community whose members prefer to live in a rarefied climate, talking to each other, subject only to "peer review" and scornful of those who translate the word "art" into "smut." (p. A21)

This drew a quick response from reader Christopher J. Gilman, who feels that the issue is not so clear-cut. Goodman's warning, though seemingly moderate in voice, he wrote,

> evokes the most damning principles of one of history's worst enemies of art . . . [and is] reminiscent of Stalin's installation of "socialist realism" as the Soviet Union's sole approved style. Its central tenet was that art had to be accessible to the masses. This was the death knell for Soviet art . . . [mark-ing] the end to decades of brilliant, innovative works of worldwide importance—which were comprehensible, un-fortunately, only to a certain elite. (*Washington Post*, October 17, 1990, p. A24)

Paul Mattick, Jr., writing in *The Nation*, offered the opinion that what advocates of restrictions on state funding have in mind is that govern-ment support should cover only art already certified as "great"—in other words, "that preserved in museums and concert halls, . . . the aesthetic component of the canon of cultural literacy promoted by such as Allan Bloom" (1990, p. 355). Indeed, the issue is not an aesthetic one, according to Mattick. He credits the emphasis on democracy and the support of multicultural diversity within public policy for bringing on much of the opposition. As Mattick sees it, the major objection has been to funding artists and institutions on the social fringe: gay and lesbian performance artists, feminist film-makers, Latino theater groups, black poets. Through the NEA, with its support of multicultural diversity, these artists have found a place inside the system. No matter how politically motivated or oppositional in form or content their work may be, given NEA support, they are within the margins of official art. Hence, for some critics, problems with the NEA are seen as stemming from the decline of decency throughout the culture and the lack of social and moral standards in making funding choices.

Moreover, he writes, much of the confusion about the role of the Endowment derives from false assumptions about our time and place:

> The argument that the state ought not to fund work repugnant to "community standards" is not a good one since it rests on the idea of a homogeneous community, with clearly demarcated standards, which does not in fact exist. ... On the other hand, the argument that art should be allowed to develop freely typically rests ... on the assumption that the development of the arts represents an interest of "society"— a unified interest that also does not exist. (October 1, 1990, p. 357)

To say that art ought not to be political is false reasoning, Mattick argues. There is no aesthetic sphere untouched by social and political meaning: the very existence of the Endowment is proof that "the generally hidden political side of the arts has existed all along. The struggle over the NEA," he says, "is a struggle for control of this political side" (p. 357).

The *Washington Post* wrote along the same lines in an editorial, pointing out that although the art world rails against restrictions and the censorship they imply, artists have colluded in politicizing the arts by accepting state and federal funding. Once artists have taken the money, the *Post* noted, " they have, at least to some degree, legitimized the intervention they so deplore" (June 29, 1989). Money has allowed the federal government access into the affairs of institutions nationwide, aiding enforcement of policy as diverse as civil rights and the 55 mph speed limit. Calling it arrogant and naive to expect otherwise, the editorial then goes on to say that by accepting government money, artists

> have entered the essential, age-old patron-client relationship, and no less than other government-assisted enterprises, they will be subjected to certain standards and demands in the name of those whose money they have taken. (June 29, 1989, p. A24)

The Present Situation

After many months of uncertainty, in the fall of 1990 the NEA was reauthorized for three years. The legislation passed by Congress leaves many aspects of the Endowmment's administrative process intact, though it increases the allocations to state and local art agencies from 20% to 35% of NEA funds by 1993 (American Assembly, 1990, p. 10). Long-term consequences of this action are as yet unclear, but the implication seems to be that the national leadership role of the Endowment will be diminished while more authority is given to the states. It remains to be seen whether states and local agencies will be required to match the increase in federal funds with new appropriations or if this allocation will merely be allowed to replace existing state funding, which is being cut in many areas.

Another significant aspect of the reauthorization package is that there will be no restrictive language regarding content, leaving decisions about obscenity to the courts. If found guilty, a grantee will have to repay any funds granted.

The reauthorization package also creates new authority for arts education programs, including funds for making education in the arts more widely available, for encouraging research to enhance teaching in the arts, and for generally facilitating work in the area of arts education (101st Congress, 1990, p. 110). Moreover, the chairperson of the NEA is charged with creating an advisory council on arts education. Of concern, however, is mention, included in the legislation, of improving "evaluation and assessment of education in the arts programs and instruction" (p. 111). This relates to the issue of technique and testing discussed in Chapter IV. It remains to be seen what action is taken on this authority.

On March 29, 1991, Doug Sonntag, who has replaced Jack Lemmon on the Dance Program staff, was asked more about the impact of the reauthorization language on the actual workings of the Dance Progam at the NEA. In response to questions regarding administrative changes within the Program, Sonntag spoke primarily about modifications in the peer panel process. For instance, Congress now requires that panels be "conflict-free":

> The Chairperson shall ensure that an individual who has a pending application for financial assistance ... or who is an employee or agent of an organization with a pending application, does not serve as a member of any panel before which such application is pending. (101st Congress, p. 123)

This new stipulation has made the system more complex and more expensive, Sonntag said. In a field like dance, dance company people are needed on the dance company panel. In order to facilitate this, the NEA has had to institute split panels, meaning that the field of company applicants will be divided between two panels, thus ensuring that no applicant serves on a panel which will be passing judgment on his/her application.

Another new specification is that

> all panels include representation of lay individuals who are knowledgeable about the arts but who are not engaged in the arts as a profession and are not members of either artists' organizations or arts organizations. (p. 122)

In response to this, Sonntag said, the Program is making an effort to "find informed people," such as those who serve on boards of directors or educators who are familiar with dance.

Other changes are less problematic. There was concern in Congress about giving out large sums of government money without being perfectly clear about how it would be spent. Sonntag affirmed that it is still possible for grantees to receive full funding thirty days in advance of incurring costs on a project, but now, when an organization requests more than two-thirds of the total sum at the beginning, a report is required during the course of the project to update the Dance Program on its progress. According to Sonntag, this stipulation applies to project grants for seasonal support, those going to arts organizations. Awards made under the category of Dance/Film/Video are for specific projects and require no interim report. Choreographer's Fellowships are considered grants to support creative time and will be distributed in lump sums.

Lillian Goldthwaite, executive director of Dance Bay Area (a California dance service organization), expressed concern about these changes in an editorial in *In Dance*. She worried that the reauthorization language calls "into question the entire concept of 'peer' review panels" (January/February 1991, p. 3). Upon examination, however, it seems that the Endowment has taken good care to preserve the peer system by installing double panels. What it has not done is to protect itself from objections of the sort raised by Kilpatrick's column on panels. Goldthwaite registers other concerns as well, including doubt about language which gives the NEA chairperson what is perhaps too much power to act as an aesthetic authority: "The Chairman of the Endowment," she writes, [is specifically charged] with the oversight of artistic excellence and merit as the criteria by which applications are reviewed. Equally, he will be responsible to ensure that all grants be awarded considering "general standards of decency and respect for the diverse beliefs and values of the American public." (1991, p. 3)

In other words, Goldthwaite questions the specific requirement that the chairperson use his or her judgment to ensure that artistic excellence and merit are the criteria by which applications are assessed, and that approved projects are generally inoffensive.

Beyond Goldthwaite's remarks, there has not yet been significant response from the dance community regarding NEA reauthorization. Nevertheless, there is much uncertainty about the situation of the arts in this country. Those involved with production, work which depends on the stability of government funding, have been especially concerned. New York Shakespeare Festival producer Joseph Papp, who rejected grant money last year rather than sign the anti-obscenity pledge, said in February 1991 that he was worried about the NEA being the only arts agency for which the administration put forward no increase in the proposed 1992 budget. "That's a slap in the face," he said. "The air is not healthy for the arts at this point. My instincts tell me there's [sic] going to be further attacks on the NEA. . . . " (Masters, 1991, p. D8).

Jefferson James remarked, in early March 1991, that as a presenter, the issues of funding and censorship were in her consciousness all the time, prompting her to re-evaluate her own role. "I used to do this work for myself," she said,

and feel secure that others would benefit. I have always been apolitical but have the sense that that's not appropriate any more. There is a difficult time ahead, and I feel I should be more of a leader now and know where I stand on these issues. What things are most important and how do we address them in the art we make and produce? (personal communication, March 4, 1991)

Speaking from the perspective of an administrator associated with the NEA, Spider Kedelsky expressed frustration, commenting on the general level of stress in the arts community due to the attacks "which have affected everyone." For the past year, he has been in Washington, coordinating the new Dance On Tour program, the latest effort to support dance company touring throughout the country. In late March 1991, he was concerned with the difficulties of instituting this kind of partnership project which requires matching funds from the states, when "State art agencies are being cut right and left." In a time of great uncertainty, he said, there has not been a unified course of action among federal and state agencies (personal communication, March 31, 1991).

Choreographers and other creative artists have had varying responses. Both Elizabeth Keen and Kathryn Posin indicated that, among some artists at least, there is the sense that art will find a way no matter what the situation. Keen views the crisis as strangely affirming: The state of affairs bears out her decision not to continue her company. "It looks like putting my company on the shelf and working in theater and opera was a good thing," she remarked in a 1991 conversation. "Given the skills I have and my assessment of the economy, my decision was appropriate. I've continued to work, choreographing however I can, while letting others do the producing" (personal communication, April 5, 1991).

Posin, writing from a ten week residency at the National Institute of the Arts in Taiwan, says that she is going back to New York University to study for a Master's degree and that she is interested in doing choreography for ballet companies. In the fall of 1990, she completed a successful work for the Milwaukee Ballet, and she has also received funding from the Ohio Arts Council to do a work on the evolution of Appalachian music. No longer performing herself, she misses having her own company, but, she writes, "the last concert we did turned out not so well because I was so busy producing, the choreography was neglected. It seems harder and less practical to keep a small company." She closes with the comment that today's economic situation is "terrible" but ultimately "meaningless. ... Since we were such fools and never did it for the economics," she writes, the "current state of affairs doesn't really change anything. I'm just as into it as ever and enjoy my foolishness, but earning a living is not always completely understood or mastered yet. ... What can I say?" (personal communication, April 2, 1991).

Stephen Greco cites Stephanie Skura as a performing artist, somewhat younger than Keen and Posin, intent on surviving in the 1990s. He notes that her attitude toward the situation has been forged under the pressure of maintaining a career in the present climate. In discussing the dilemma of accepting money from sources she does not sanction, Skura's position is that these days pragmatic concerns overwhelm issues of social consciousness. "Is there any organization you can name that gives money to the arts, that isn't involved in things you don't approve of?" she asks.

According to Greco, Skura spends considerable time raising money instead of making dances, an ironic situation she accepts as necessary to retain the purity of her work. "Sometimes I feel that I just can't keep begging for money on a daily basis," she says,

> and that I should consider the "prostitution" of commercial work, which I've always avoided. It takes so much out of me just to stay in touch with funding people; I try to remain optimistic for them when I actually have no idea how I'll be able to go on. But then I do go on. (1991, p. 12)

Artists, historically, have not had a strong track record in defending the arts. After Ronald Reagan's budget cuts to the NEA in 1981, the arts community breathed a sigh of relief and absorbed the difference, feeling thankful that the situation was not worse. Then we waited for things to right themselves (FEDAPT, p. 10). The political power base the NEA had enjoyed under previous administrations had been undercut, however, and under Reagan, the stage was set for a major debate over government arts funding.

During the crisis of the past two years, the art world has borne out FEDAPT's description, discussed earlier in this chapter, of a heavily regulated industry facing changes in its working environment. In general, the response has been uncritical support of the Endowment and its policies, with curtailment of funding likened to censorship and an infringement on First Amendment rights of free speech. At the same time, however, in confronting the political process head on, supporters of the arts have revealed a deficiency in knowledge about the system and a general lack of preparedness to compete for public support. In addition, in trying to coalesce around commonly shared goals, fractures have occurred in the arts community itself, brought on by hitherto unacknowledged differences in objectives and perspectives (American Assembly, 1990, p. 11). It is clear that, although the Endowment endures—at least for the present—the struggle for survival has raised many issues which must be faced before there can be resolution.

And still, there has been little from the art world in the way of pondering the function of the NEA, or the uses of art in American politics, or the ubiquitous question of whether funding is better used for preservation or creation, or most important, who decides? This unsettled time might be seen as an occasion to rethink the position on the arts, for those in the arts to re-establish priorities, take on the politics of the art world itself, and to redefine the meaning of words like "professional" and "success," given today's realities.

The NEA serves as the agent of public affirmation of the arts, and as such, it must be defended. But instead of blindly supporting the agency, this time could be used to grasp the implications of its guidelines and policies, and to fully understand the part artists play in determining their role in American society. Paul Mattick, Jr. closes his article in *The Nation* with a quote from an editorial in the *New Art Examiner* which seems particularly apt. "While it is necessary to rally the field against censorship to the right," it reads,

> why is it not necessary to rally the field against censorship by insiders? Why shouldn't we deal with the abuses of a closed panel system? Why shouldn't we examine the cronyism of organizations, artist's spaces, and publications, who year after year receive NEA funding, and who supply the NEA with peer review panel members and site visitors? (p. 358)

The discussion opened up by Jesse Helms and his friends can be made an occasion to consider the nature of art and the relationship of artists to it. The crisis of the past two years has created the opportunity to gain a voice. Or many voices. Is it not time for artists to assume a place in the dialogue on policy which bears so strongly on their lives and their work?

Bibliography

Adler, J. (1981, March 16). The arts under Reagan's ax. *Newsweek*, pp. 28–31.

Allyn, A. (1987, January–February). Arts advocacy. *American Dance Guild Newsletter*, p. 8.

American Assembly. (1990, November 8–11). *The arts & government: Questions for the nineties.* Columbia University, New York: author.

Banes, S. (1983). *Democracy's body: Judson Dance Theater 1962–64.* Ann Arbor: UMI Research Press.

Banes, S. (1987). *Terpsichore in Sneakers.* Middletown, CT: Wesleyan University Press.

Baumol, H. & Baumol, W. J. (Eds.). (1984). *Inflation and the performing arts.* New York, London: New York University Press.

Baumol, W. J. & Bowen, W. G. (1966). *Performing arts: The economic dilemma.* New York: The Twentieth Century Fund.

Belenky, M. F., Clinchy, B. M., Goldberger, N. R., & Tarule, J. M. (1986). *Women's ways of knowing: The development of self, voice, and mind.* New York: Basic Books, Inc., Publishers.

Biddle, L. (1984). Our government's support for the arts: Nourishment or drought?

In P. A. McFate (Ed.), *The Annals of the American Academy of Political and Social Science: Paying for Culture, 471* (pp. 89–101). Beverly Hills: Sage Publications.

Brooks, B. (1991, April 8). Letters to the editor. *The Washington Post.*

Bromberg, C. S. (1981). Dance as commodity. *Dance Scope, 15,* 8–18.

Buckroyd, J. (1988a, April). *Dancing Times,* pp. 647–649.

Buckroyd, J. (1988b, July). *The emotional needs of the young performer.* Paper presented at the Dance and the Child International Conference, London.

Cash, D. (1987, July 17). In the African folk art tradition. *The Boston Globe.*

Catanoso, J. (1988, December 16). N. C. School of Arts caught up in drama. *Greensboro News & Record,* pp. A1, A12.

Chin, D. (1975). Add some more cornstarch, or the plot thickens: Yvonne Rainer's *Work 1961–73. Dance Scope, 9,* 50–64.

101st Congress. (1990, October 16). *H.R. 5769.* Washington, DC: author.

Cohen, S. J. (1966). Introduction: The caterpillar's question. In S. J. Cohen (Ed.), *The modern dance: Seven statements of belief.* Middletown, CT: Wesleyan University Press.

Croce, A. (1988, November 28). Profiles: II—the prodigal. *The New Yorker,* pp. 42–66.

Cunningham, M. (1985). *The dancer and the dance.* New York, London: Marion Boyars.

de Mille, A. (1952). *Dance to the piper.* Boston: Little, Brown and Company.

de Mille, A. (1980). *America dances.* New York: Macmillan Publishing Co., Inc.

Dubin, S. C. (1987). *Bureaucratizing the muse: Public funds and the cultural worker.* Chicago, London: University of Chicago Press.

Duncan, Irma (1959). *Isadora Duncan: Pioneer in the art of dance.* New York: The New York Public Library.

Duncan, Isadora. (1983). The dance of the future. In R. Copeland & M. Cohen (Eds.), *What is dance: Readings in theory and criticism* (pp. 262–264). Oxford: Oxford University Press.

Dunn, A. (1991, February). Facing the new realities: North Carolina arts in the nineties (Part two). *The Arts Journal, 16,* pp. 10–13.

Dunning, J. (1985). *"But first a school": The first fifty years of the School of the American Ballet.* New York: Elisabeth Sifton Books—Viking.

Dunning, J. (1987, January 18). Dance: Kathryn Posin. *New York Times,* p. A50.

Eginton, M. (1991, April). The eye of the observer. *Dance Ink, 2,* pp. 10–11.

FEDAPT. (1991, August 15). Letter from director Nello McDaniel.

FEDAPT. (1991). *1989–1990 Annual Report: The quiet crisis in the arts.* New York: author.

Forti, S. (1974). *Handbook in motion.* Halifax: The press of the Nova Scotia College of Art and Design, and New York: New York University Press.

Gadan, F. & Maillard, R. (Eds.). (1959). *Dictionary of modern ballet.* New York: Tudor Publishing Company.

Gadlin, H. (1977). Private lives and public order: A critical view of the history of intimate relations in the United States. In G. Levinger & H. L. Raush (Eds.), *Close relationships* (pp. 33–72). Amherst: University of Massachusetts Press.

Gamble, J. (1988, December). [Conversation with John Gamble, Jr.].

Gans, H. J. (1974). *Popular culture and high culture: An analysis and evaluation of taste.* New York: Basic Books, Inc., Publishers.

Gilman, C. J. (1990, October 17). Letters to the editor. *The Washington Post,* p. A24.

Goldthwaite, L. (1991, January/February). From the executive director. *In Dance,* p. 3.

Goodman, E. (1990, October 9). A warning from the Mapplethorpe trial. *The Washington Post,* p. A21.

Goody, K. (1984). Arts funding: Growth and change between 1963 and 1983. In P. A. McFate (Ed.), *The Annals of the American Academy of Political and Social Science: Paying for Culture, 471* (pp. 89–101). Beverly Hills: Sage Publications.

Greco, S. (1991, April). What's a poor artist to do? *Dance Ink, 2,* pp. 12–13.

Haacke, H. (1981, Summer). Working conditions. *Art Forum,* pp. 56–61.

Hanna, J. L. (1987a). Gender "language" onstage: Moves, new moves and countermoves. *Journal of the Washington Academy of Sciences, 77,* 18–25.

Hanna, J. L. (1987b). Patterns of dominance. *The Drama Review, 14,* 24–47.

Hardy, C. (1986, April). At twenty, the NEA attracts an alliance of big spenders. *Dance Magazine,* pp. 76–79.

Harris, D. (1989, January 31). Dance: An American iconoclast in Paris. *The Wall Street Journal,* p. A16.

Hart, F. E. (1989, August 22). Contemporary art is perverted art. *The Washington Post,* p. A19.

Henry, W. A. III. (1990, July 16). You can take this grant and ... *Time,* p. 85.

Hoffa, H. E. (1981, October). The arts and the federal government: Gambit or end-game? *Design for Arts in Education,* pp. 4–18.

Horosko, M. (1988, November). Education. *Dance Magazine,* pp. 68–69.

Hughes, R. (1989, August 14). A loony parody of cultural democracy. *Time,* p. 82.

Humphrey, D. (1966, Spring). New dance: An unfinished autobiography. *Dance Perspectives 25*, pp. 9–77.

Innes, S. (1988, Winter). The teaching of ballet. *Writings in Dance, 3*, pp. 37–47.

James, J. (1988, November 27). [Interview with Jefferson James].

James, J. (1991, March 5). [Conversation with Jefferson James].

Jameson, F. (1984). Postmodernism, or the cultural logic of late capitalism. *New Left Review, 146*, 53–93.

Joyce, M. S. (1984). Government funding of culture: What price the arts? In P. A. McFate (Ed.), *The Annals of the American Academy of Political and Social Science: Paying for Culture, 471*, (pp. 27–33). Beverly Hills: Sage Publications.

Kastor, E. (1991, February 5). Bush budget slights NEA. *The Washington Post*, p. C1.

Kedelsky, S. (1988, September 23). [Interview with Spider Kedelsky].

Kedelsky, S. (1991, March 31). [Conversation with Spider Kedelsky].

Keen, E. (1988, October 14). [Interview with Elizabeth Keen].

Keen, E. (1991, April 5). [Conversation with Elizabeth Keen].

Keller, E. B. (1984). The public and the arts. In P. A. McFate (Ed.), *The Annals of the American Academy of Political and Social Science: Paying for Culture, 471*. Beverly Hills: Sage Publications.

Kilpatrick, J. J. (1990, March 11). Paying taxes to be offended. *Greensboro News & Record*, p. E4.

Kilpatrick, J. J. (1991, March 24). When it comes to the NEA, grants are all in the family. *Greensboro News & Record*, p. B4.

King, E. (1978). *Transformations: A memoir by Eleanor King—the Humphrey-Weidman Era*. Brooklyn: Dance Horizons.

Kirkland, G. (1986). *Dancing on my grave*. Garden City, New York: Doubleday & Company, Inc.

Kogan, J. (1987). *Nothing but the best: The struggle for perfection at The Julliard School*. New York: Random House.

Kraus, R. G. & Chapman, S. A. (1981). *History of the dance in art and education*, Englewood Cliffs, NJ: Prentice-Hall.

Kriegsman, A. M. (1987, April 26). Liz Lerman, democrat of dance. *The Washington Post*, pp. G1, G7.

Lawson, W. J. (Ed.). (1988). *88/89 College guide*. New York: Dance Magazine, Inc.

Lawson, W. J. (Ed.). (1988). *Stern's performing arts directory 1989*. New York: DMInc.

Lemmon, J. R. (1988, October 20). [Interview with Jack R. Lemmon].

Lipman, S. (1985, January/February). Cultural policy: Whither America, whither government? *Design for Arts in Education*, pp. 19–25.

Lipman, S. (1989, January/February). The NEA: Looking back, and looking ahead. *Design for Arts in Education*, pp. 2–9.

Lowry, W. M. (1978). The past twenty years, and Conclusion. In W. M. Lowry (Ed.), *The performing arts and American society* (pp. 3–26, 198–210). Englewood Cliffs, NJ: Prentice-Hall, Inc.

Masters, K. (1991, February 21). NEA drops contested grant oath. *The Washington Post*, pp. D1, D8.

Mattick, P., Jr. (1990, October 1). Arts and the state. *The Nation, 251*, pp. 348–358.

Mazo, J. H. (1978). Modern dance. In W. M. Lowry (Ed.), *The performing arts and American society* (pp. 76–95). Englewood Cliffs, NJ: Prentice-Hall, Inc.

Mazo, J. H. (1984, July/August). Ailey & company. *Horizon*, pp. 18–24.

McDonagh, D. (1970). *The rise and fall and rise of modern dance*. New York: Outerbridge & Dienstfrey.

McDonagh, D. (1973). *Martha Graham: A biography*. New York, Washington: Praeger Publishers.

McDonagh, D. (1976). *The complete guide to modern dance*. Garden City, New York: Doubleday & Company, Inc.

Meta-Marketing Panel. (1988, March 20). Presented by Movement Research Inc., New York, NY.

National Association of Schools of Dance. (1985). *A brochure describing the functions of the association*. Reston, VA: author.

National Association of Schools of Dance. (1987). *Handbook 1988–1989*. Reston, VA: author.

National Endowment for the Arts. (1967 through 1988). *Annual Report*. Washington, DC: author.

National Endowment for the Arts. (1987 through 1990). *Dance Application Guidelines*. Washington, DC: author.

National Endowment for the Arts. (1988). *Five-year planning document 1990–1994*. Washington, DC: author.

National Endowment for the Arts. (1988, May). *Toward civilization: A report on arts education*. Washington, DC: author.

Netzer, D. (1978). *The subsidized muse*. Cambridge: Cambridge University Press.

Netzer, D. (1986, May). Dance in New York: Market and subsidy changes. *American Economic Review*, pp. 15–19.

Nikolais, A. (1985). Modern dance today. In N. S. Fichter (Ed.), *Dance administration: Themes and directions* (p. 5). Allerton House, Monticello, Illinois: Conference on Dance Administration.

Page, R. (1984). *Class: Notes on dance classes around the world 1915–1980.* Princeton, NJ: Princeton Book Company, Publishers.

Pankratz, D. B. (1986, July/August). Aesthetic welfare, government, and educational policy. *Design for Arts in Education,* pp. 12–24.

People in the news. (1988, September 20). *Greensboro News & Record,* p. A3.

Posin, K. (1988, October 16). [Interview with Kathyrn Posin].

Posin, K. (1991, April 2). [Personal communication].

Rainer, Y. (1974). *Work 1961–73.* Halifax: The Press of the Nova Scotia College of Art and Design, and New York: New York University Press.

Ruyter, N. L. C. (1979). *Reformers and visionaries.* New York: Dance Horizons.

Salisbury, W. (1988, November 21). Troupe lacks polish, but director shines. *The Plain Dealer.*

Sande, R. (1989, February). [Conversation with Rona Sande].

Schulman, S. (1991, Winter/Spring). What ideals guide our actions? *Movement Research Performance Journal #2,* p. 3.

Shapiro, L. (1989, April 10). Where are all the men? *Newsweek,* pp. 62–63.

Silver, D. B. (1988, May). [Interview with Dorothy Berea Silver].

Sonntag, D. (1991, March 29). [Conversation with Doug Sonntag].

Steadman, T. (1988, October 30). Much ado about the arts. *Greensboro News & Record,* pp. H1, H5.

Stinson, S., Blumenfeld-Jones, D., & Van Dyke, J. Voices of adolescent students: An interpretive study of meaning in dance. In S. H. Fraleigh (Ed.), *Proceedings of the International CORD Conference on Dance and Culture,* July 1988. Toronto. (pp. 174–184).

Stodelle, E. (1978). *The dance technique of Doris Humphrey and its creative potential.* London: Dance Books Ltd.

Stodelle, E. (1984). *Deep song: The dance story of Martha Graham.* New York: Schirmer Books.

Sussman, L. (1984, Fall). Anatomy of the dance company boom, 1968–1980. *Dance Research Journal, 16,* pp. 23–28.

Sussman, L. (1990, Spring). Recruitment patterns; Their impact on ballet and modern dance. *Dance Research Journal, 22,* pp. 21–28.

Swidler, A. (1980). Love and adulthood in American culture. In N. J. Smelser & E. H. Erikson (Eds.), *Themes of love and work in adulthood* (pp. 120–150). Cambridge, MA: Harvard University Press.

Taylor, P. (1987). *Private domain*. New York: Alfred A. Knopf.

Terry, W. (1971). *The dance in America*. New York: Harper & Row Publishers.

Urice, J. K. (1991, January/February). Artistic expression and government support: New perspectives on old issues. *Design for Arts in Education*, pp. 2–8.

Useem, M. (1976, July/August). Government patronage of science and art in America. *American Behavioral Scientist*, pp. 785–804.

Valeriano, L. L. (1991, March 22). Pennsylvania Ballet, other companies face swan song if funds don't rise. *The Wall Street Journal*, p. B10B.

The Washington Post. (1989, June 29). . . . And the Corcoran mess. p. A24.

Wheeler, M. (1986). *New dance in a New Deal era*. Paper presented at AAHPERD Research Consortium, AAHPERD National Convention, Cincinnati.

Wicker, T. (1990, July 6). 1st amendment's spreading chill. *Greensboro News & Record*, p. A15.

Winfield, L. (1990, July 9). Letters to the editor. *Greensboro News & Record*, p. A8.

Woolf, J. (1981). *The social production of art*. New York: St. Martin's Press.